Paul Pierce: The Inspiring Story of One of Basketball's Greatest Small Forwards

An Unauthorized Biography

By: Clayton Geoffreys

Visit my website at www.claytongeoffreys.com
Cover photo by Keith Allison is licensed under CC BY 2.0 / modified from original

Table of Contents

Foreword

Whenever anyone thinks about the Boston Celtics franchise in the first decade of the new millennium, they do not have to think for long before they bring up the name, Paul Pierce. Pierce played for the Celtics from 1998 until 2013 and was an integral player for the franchise. With the help of All-Stars Kevin Garnett, Ray Allen, and Rajon Rondo, Paul Pierce and his teammates revitalized a once forgotten franchise and ushered in a new era of Boston basketball. While Pierce has since moved on to other teams since the 2008 NBA Championship run and the Big Three era, there is no question that Paul Pierce and his legacy will forever be linked to the Boston Celtics. Thank you for purchasing *Paul Pierce: The Inspiring Story of One of Basketball's Greatest Small Forwards*. In this unauthorized biography, we will learn Paul Pierce's incredible life story and impact on the game of basketball. Hope you enjoy and if you do, please do not forget to leave a review!

Also, check out my website at claytongeoffreys.com to join my exclusive list where I let you know about my latest books. To thank you for your purchase, you can go to my site to download a free copy of *33 Life Lessons: Success Principles, Career Advice & Habits of Successful People*. In the book, you'll learn from some of the greatest thought leaders of different industries on what it takes to become successful and how to live a great life.

Cheers,

Clayton Geoffreys

Visit me at www.claytongeoffreys.com

Introduction

Throughout the long history of the NBA, the league has seen its share of big shot takers and shot makers. We have heard about Jerry West's penchant for making and hitting big shots in clutch situations during the earlier years of the NBA. There is no wonder why he is the league's logo and the very first player to win the Finals MVP award. Fast-forward to the 80's, and you will hear about Magic Johnson and Larry Bird fighting for league supremacy by playing and performing at their best in big-game situations. A few years after them, Michael Jordan became a household name throughout his career when it came to making big shots and winning big games. His clutch plays have made him one of the most famous basketball players in the world. During Mike's prime, Reggie Miller also rose up to break hearts by hitting big shots. The new millennium dawned, and we have seen guys like Kobe Bryant, Dirk Nowitzki, LeBron James, and Dwyane Wade among others making and hitting clutch shots. In today's generation, we have players like Stephen Curry, Kevin Durant, and James Harden draining big shots. However, there seems to be one name that often finds itself missing in conversations about the biggest shot makers of the NBA despite having delivered time and time again for almost two decades. That great NBA player is Paul Pierce.

Scoring is the name of the game, and almost nobody else in the world can match up to how Paul Pierce puts buckets in the hoop night in and night out. However, when he came out of college in 1998 to join the NBA, he was not one of the most heralded prospects. He was a good player, but nobody saw what Pierce was truly capable of as a future star player. Despite that, Paul immediately showed that he could deliver buckets and hit big shots in just his rookie season. Pierce quickly became a star to build on for the storied franchise of the Boston Celtics.

Playing in Boston was not so simple for Paul Pierce. He grew up in Inglewood, California, which was just a short drive away from Los Angeles. As such, Pierce grew up watching and idolizing the Los Angeles Lakers. He was inspired to play basketball by the Lakers, and he wanted to be a Laker himself. However, the Lakers were bitter rivals with the Celtics. That made playing for Boston morally difficult for Paul Pierce. And even when Pierce had warmed up to the Boston franchise, bearing the weight of the team with the most NBA championships in NBA history was not easy for Pierce. He was a solitary star playing for a team whose fans had a lot of expectations for the Celtics' best players. Though Paul had figured himself in the playoffs several times in the early days of his NBA career, he would never have the chance to win the most coveted prize in all of basketball – the NBA championship.

Though Paul Pierce's early days in the NBA were tainted with mediocrity and early exits in the playoffs, it was not because of a lack of effort on the part of the superstar small forward. Pierce was arguably one of the best players in his position at that time. At the small forward position, no other NBA player could match how Pierce could score in bunches with his unique combination of post moves, dribble pull-ups, and outside shots. Because of Paul's ability to score and his skills in torching other teams, Shaquille O'Neal, who was playing with the rival Los Angeles Lakers at the time, would coin Pierce's ever popular nickname, "The Truth." That came up after Pierce put up 42 points on the Lakers in 2001.[i] Since then, The Truth had always been a household name in the All-Star Game while finishing seasons as a part of an All-NBA Team. He was that good. However, a championship ring and a chance to play for it were always eluding Paul Pierce.

In 2007, everything drastically changed for Paul Pierce and the Boston Celtics. Two other superstars, namely Kevin Garnett and Ray Allen, were growing tired of how their respective teams could not deliver good supporting casts for a possible chance at the championship. As such, the Celtics made moves to acquire both players to recreate a Boston trio of NBA superstars affectionately called "The Big Three." The new Boston Big Three would go on to dominate the league despite the fact that they had only played together for less than a season. The trio's unselfishness and chemistry led them to the best record in the NBA in 2008. They would go on to beat the rival Los Angeles Lakers in six games in the NBA Finals.

After winning the NBA title in 2008, Pierce and company would go back to the NBA Finals in 2010 only to be beaten by the Lakers in seven intensely close games. Because of how Paul Pierce and his two other superstar teammates revived the Boston Celtics franchise, the top-tier rivalry between the Celtics and the Lakers was renewed for even just a short span of time. Nevertheless, Pierce has hit countless big shots on his way to a championship in 2008 and a second NBA Finals appearance in 2010.

Shortly after the loss to the Lakers in 2010, the Boston Big Three was disbanded when Ray Allen accepted a role on the Miami Heat roster. Despite strong performances in the playoffs after the trio was disbanded, Pierce and Celtics would never see the light of the NBA Finals ever again. It would not take long for the Boston Celtics to totally break up the championship team by sending Paul Pierce and Kevin Garnett over to the rebuilding

Brooklyn Nets for a chance to rebuild the team itself. Though Pierce knew he wanted to stay as a Celtic for the entirety of his career, he did what was best for the team.

The Truth went on to play for the Nets, Washington Wizards, and Los Angeles Clippers as a journeyman role player after he left Boston. Despite the decreased role of the aging Paul Pierce, his part in making big shots was diminished. A good example of that was when Paul Pierce banked in a big shot that won the game in the 2015 playoffs when they faced off against the Atlanta Hawks in Game 3 of their series. When asked if he "called bank" in that shot, Pierce went on to say he "called game."[ii] That is significant confidence for a big player known for his knack for hitting big shots. Though Pierce's career is in its twilight, history says that we should never sleep on his ability to come up suddenly to hit the biggest shot of a big game.

Chapter 1: Childhood and Early Years

The NBA champion player known as "The Truth" was born as Paul Anthony Pierce on October 13, 1977. Pierce initially grew up in Oakland, California until his mom Lorraine Hosey relocated the family to Inglewood as she had to go to Los Angeles every day to work two jobs since she was a single mother raising three children. As such, Paul never knew the identity of his father and grew up raised almost solely by his mother.

Though Paul Pierce grew up without a father figure in the family, he grew up well thanks to the good influence of his two older half-brothers, Jamal and Stephen. Though the older brothers would help to raise Paul in other ways, the best way that they helped their younger brother was through sports. The Inglewood neighborhood they lived in was not the friendliest as gangs and drugs were apparent in the streets. Sports were the best way to keep the siblings out of trouble. Lorraine, of course, loved the idea of keepings her boys out of the streets. Hence, she encouraged her kids to give all that they could towards athletic developments.[iii]

While Stephen ventured out to playing baseball as a young boy, Jamal and Paul were more interested in playing basketball. Of course, as a young boy living in Inglewood, Paul Pierce's basketball imagination was captured by the Showtime 80's edition of the Los Angeles Lakers, who played at The Forum, which was located in Inglewood. The Lakers were arguably the most entertaining team to watch during the 80's era of basketball. As such, it was so easy for the Lakers of that era to inspire young boys to venture into the sport of basketball. Paul was one of those young kids. He would remember that he was about six years old when he saw the Lakers versus the Celtics in an NBA Finals series back in the 80's.[iv] That was when he decided that he wanted to play the game at a high level.

As a mischievous basketball fan, Paul Pierce would always sneak into The Forum to watch Lakers games. It also helped that his family was living in the shadow of the arena where the Lakers played back in those days. Paul would just have to walk a few blocks down the road to reach The Forum. Seeing the Lakers and watching basketball played at the highest level in person helped his motivation to become better at the sport. He even once envisioned being the next Magic Johnson like most kids living near or in Los Angeles back in those days. Of course, he would not have snuck into those Laker games without a little help. Paul and a few other kids from the neighborhood were able to see the Lakers live in person with the support of Scott

Collins, a detective in Inglewood who would sometimes work as Security in The Forum.[iv]

Collins was also sidelining as a coach for youth basketball programs in Inglewood back in those days. Paul Pierce had the pleasure of working under him while he served as the future basketball superstar's coach in organized basketball camps and tournaments sponsored by the police force of Inglewood. Because Paul grew up without a father, Collins was the closest thing to one for him and many other children in the area. With Collins' help, Pierce developed into an excellent youth basketball player. Though he was a little chubby as a kid, it did not stop him from doing well on the floor. He could shoot the three ball pretty well even back in those days.[iii] As he grew a little older, Paul became more athletic as a kid. Of course, he did not get to that point naturally. With the proper training and exercises, Pierce became quicker and more athletic as a young boy. Collins would even go on to say that Paul Pierce was a good athlete that could pretty much play any sport.[iv]

Basketball was simply Paul Pierce's first love when he was a kid. He would sometimes even sneak out to play basketball as a way to escape reality or as a way to have fun whenever he was being punished by his mother. Pierce would call the sport his "peace of mind." He would even go further to call it "his church" because it was the one thing that gave him mental and spiritual clarity when everything else did not seem right. It also helped that Paul Pierce had a lot of idols to look up to when he was at that age. First of all, there was no denying that he loved Magic Johnson. But he also deeply idolized Larry Bird, even though the Celtic legend was playing for the Lakers' rival city. Lastly, like most kids that grew up in the 80's and 90's, he imitated Michael Jordan on the basketball court. He wanted to dunk and make basketball look easy like Jordan did. However, Magic was still his favorite player as a boy because he was the one player that made basketball inspirational with the way that he led the Lakers in the 80's.[v]

Chapter 2: High School Career

Paul Pierce enrolled in Inglewood High School in 1991. At that time, he was a shooting guard that stood less than 5'8". Looking at Paul Pierce back in those days, you would wonder why and how he became a basketball superstar. He was not the tallest guy on the floor. He also seemed a little chubby for his age. By all means, he was an average Joe who simply had some basketball skills to compromise his lack of height, build, and athleticism.[iv]

When he tried for the varsity team of Inglewood High, Paul Pierce received one of the most devastating news of his basketball career. In his freshman year in high school, he was cut from the varsity team.[iv] He did not make it, especially with his lack of size and athleticism at the shooting guard position. Paul was going up against teenagers that had developed into their athletic bodies. They could run the floor twice as fast as Pierce could. However, Paul was not the only future basketball superstar that got cut from the varsity team. His idol Michael Jordan was also a youngster that got cut from the high school team back in the day. But that did not stop him from developing into arguably the greatest basketball player of all time. After that fateful day, MJ went immediately to his room and cried all day. Mike eventually got back on the horse and worked hard on his game to become a better player, not just in high school or college, but historically.

However, Paul initially wanted to give up on Inglewood after he got cut. Though he was a member of the junior varsity team, the best option he wanted to take was to transfer to another school to get a chance to play for the team. He knew Inglewood High had a better team and program, but he could not bear the thought of not making the varsity team. Then his brothers intervened. Jamal and Stephen, who were both good athletes back in those days, told Paul never to give up and to work harder than he ever did before. They would tell him that a person could never run away from competition if he wanted to become one of the best. The only way to become the best is to face competition head on by becoming better and by working harder. Paul Pierce would go on to say that his brothers' words were the best advice he has ever received in his entire life.

Hyped up and motivated by his older brothers, Paul Pierce got back on his horse and worked tirelessly to hone his craft. The young teenager would go to the gym as early as five o'clock in the morning. As a member of the junior varsity team, Paul Pierce did not slack off, even though he played off the bench. In one game, Pierce would only play five minutes as a reserve, but he was the one who delivered the win to his team via a buzzer-beating game-winner. Paul Pierce would call that moment his favorite childhood memory as it was the first time he was swarmed by his teammates for a memorable victory shot.[v]

By the time Paul Pierce was done with his freshman season as a member of the junior varsity team, luck had played a big hand. Before his sophomore season, Pierce barely made it to the varsity squad as his hard work paid off. However, he was still playing off the bench as he was not as good as the other teens at that time. The coaching staff was even tempted to put him back on the JV team because he did not contribute much to the main squad. That was when luck came into play. The Christmas holidays came, and several players were out of town to enjoy the break.

Inglewood head coach Patrick Roy would still play the team in the tournament that season. With some of the main guns unavailable, Inglewood was down big in one during the tournament. Succumbing to the seemingly inevitable defeat, Roy put in Paul Pierce to play mop-up duty. The then-5'8" shooting guard suddenly shined. Pierce took the game over and singlehandedly brought Inglewood back from a big deficit to win the game. Roy would say that Paul had 21 points, six rebounds, and six assists off the bench as he was a one-man wrecking crew for Inglewood in that win. That was when Roy decided that Paul Pierce belonged on the varsity team. Not only had he secured a spot in the main squad, he was also given a slot in the starting five.[iv] Even as the older players came back from break, Paul never lost his place in the team rotation.

In his third year in high school, Paul Pierce worked even harder as the go-to guy of Inglewood High School. His skills were vastly improving as he got used to the fact that he was already the best player on the team after riding the bench for most of his first two years in high school. Paul's body would also cooperate with his skills. As his skills were improving, so were his physical attributes. Pierce advanced to a height of more than 6 feet tall. He also lost a lot of weight as he began to move quicker and more athletically on the floor. Pierce led the team to a division title that season.[iv]

Paul Pierce skills and his body did not stop improving. By the time he got to his senior and final year in high school, Pierce was already about 6'6". Though he was already a legitimate go-to-guy in his junior year, it was in his fourth year when he started to shine as a future NBA prospect. Paul Pierce averaged 24.5 points, 11.5 rebounds, and four assists in his senior year in high school. In a state where basketball was played at its finest among high school players, Pierce was arguably the best

15

prospect heading into college that season. He was the California Player of the Year in 1995 as he joined the teenage version of future NBA All-Stars Kevin Garnett, Stephon Marbury, and Vince Carter to play in the McDonald's All-American Game that year.

Several college teams started recruiting Paul Pierce to play for their program come the following season. Despite the good crop of recruitment offers, Paul narrowed it down to the University of California, Los Angeles and the University of Kansas. Pierce originally wanted to stay in Southern California to play for UCLA as it was close to him. However, he did not like the busy city life of living in Los Angeles. Paul also said that going to UCLA meant that he had to remain at home living with his mom. He did not like the idea of being a mama's boy. Pierce wanted to grow up as his own independent man. Hence, he chose to go to Kansas to play for the Jayhawks.

One other factor that led Pierce to go to Kansas was how head coach Roy Williams recruited the young teenager. Williams did not sugarcoat anything to Pierce. He told the youngster from Inglewood that he would be treated like everyone else on the team and that he needed to work just as hard, if not harder, than his teammates. Though Williams would also say that Pierce had the potential to become the best player on the team, the caveat was that Paul had to work intensely hard to earn that role.[iv] Williams' recruitment pitch was not too shabby, either. Four of their starters were returning the following season, but they lost their starting small forward. What they did was cut a piece of cardboard into five pieces. They gave Paul the four corner pieces and sent the center piece a few days later. The center piece was a star, and it had Pierce's photo on it. They meant to tell Paul that he was the missing piece of the Kansas puzzle.[vi]

Chapter 3: College Career

Paul Pierce joined the Kansas Jayhawks as a good recruit that was able to hold his own against older and more experienced players. Though Coach Roy Williams had previously told Pierce that he had to work harder to become the best player on the team, it did not take a lot of effort or time for Paul to secure a permanent spot in the starting five. Though Pierce was not the designated go-to guy in his first year in college, he did well for the Jayhawks as a scorer. It was in that year when Paul Pierce realized that he had potential. In his freshman season, he finally knew and understood that with more hard work and improvements, he could make it into the professional league. After that, he would not slack off and he dreamt of playing in the NBA.[v]

It also turned out that Paul Pierce was the missing piece of the Kansas Jayhawks' starting five. Though he was not yet the best player on the team, he earned his minutes, and he earned his numbers. Paul averaged 11.9 points, 5.3 rebounds, and 1.3 steals while shooting 42% from the field in about 25 minutes of action in 34 games. When the Big 12 was still the Big 8, Paul Pierce and the Jayhawks went on to win the Conference title that season and he proved to be the crucial piece that Kansas needed to contend for the national title. However, they would eventually lose to the Syracuse Orangemen in the Elite Eight of the NCAA Tournament.[vi] Nevertheless, Pierce won the Big 8 Conference Rookie of the Year award along with Chauncey Billups.

At that time, Pierce was still a raw prospect that did not get a lot of national media coverage. However, some scouts and analysts believed he had more potential than some of his fellow rookies that season. Had he joined the NBA Draft in 1996, he would have been drafted in the first round. He would have been one of the legendary figures that belonged to the Draft Class of 1996. However, Pierce believed he still had a lot more work to do before trying his hand at the NBA Draft.

It turned out that Paul Pierce's decision to stay longer with the Kansas Jayhawks was not wrong. He put in a lot of hard work in the offseason and looked to be a vital piece of the Jayhawk system. But he was not just an important part. Instead, he was the most important piece as he came back to become the best player on the Kansas roster during the 1996-97 season. Though the competition grew tougher as the Big 8 became the Big 12, Paul Pierce was even bigger. He led the Jayhawks to another Conference championship as Kansas would merely lose one game throughout the whole season. Because of that, Pierce had made Kansas the top-seeded team in the entire nation heading into the NCAA tournament.

In 28 minutes of action in 36 games, Pierce averaged 16.3 points, 6.8 rebounds, and 1.7 steals that season while upping his efficiency to about 49% from the floor. Despite the success that Paul Pierce and the Jayhawks were seeing that season, he was merely Third Team All-Conference that season. Nevertheless, Paul Pierce went on to put on a show as he was named the Big 12 Conference Most Valuable Player that season.

As the top-seeded team in the United States that season, the Kansas Jayhawks were the title favorites in the NCAA tournament. They made it all the way to the Sweet 16. However, it would seem that the Jayhawks could not even make it as far as they had the previous season. The Arizona Wildcats would beat the Kansas Jayhawks and would eventually win the national title a few games later. But the loss was not because of Pierce. Paul was brilliant in that game as he put up 27 points and 11 rebounds. An Arizona coach, Lute Olson, was quite impressed by how Pierce almost singlehandedly defeated the Wildcats. He called Pierce the "best player they faced in the NCAA tournament."[vi]

After the defeat, Paul Pierce was deeply disappointed with how the team ended up exiting the competition early despite their superior seed. It was the hardest the team had worked at in a very long time, but they still fell short of a national title. Instead of dwelling on the loss, Paul would use the disappointment as the necessary fuel to become better. However, it was also at that time when many scouts believed Pierce was ready to go to the professionals as a no-brainer lottery pick. To silence the rumors, Paul would announce in an exhibition game that he was coming back to Kansas for at least one more season as he wanted to look forward to a more successful Jayhawks run for the 1997-98 season.

Paul Pierce and the Jayhawks proved that the previous season was not a fluke. They came into the 1997-98 season as dominant as ever. Pierce continued to score at a career rate for Kansas that season. However, he also learned when and how to involve his teammates in tight situations. He was growing up to become an unselfish leader that also knew when to make the right shots. Paul Pierce also showed the entire nation what he was capable of as a clutch big shot maker in big shot situations.

In a blowout win against Texas, Pierce was hobbled with ailments. He injured his knee and ankle, but was still able to perform big. He finished the game with 31 points. He then had the same amount of points in a win against Oklahoma. Sensing that Paul Pierce had played his final home game for the Kansas Jayhawks, the home crowd, who never saw a loss at home in 60 games, chanted for Paul to stay with Kansas until his senior year.[iii] Despite the pleading cries, Paul Pierce would never play in Kansas again after that win versus Oklahoma.

Paul Pierce once again led Kansas to the Conference Title. With averages of 20.4 points, 6.7 rebounds, 2.6 assists, and 1.1 steals while shooting 51.3% from the floor, Pierce was a no-brainer for his second consecutive Conference MVP award. He was also named as a member of the All-American First Team. He would once again lead the Kansas Jayhawks towards a bright future in the NCAA tournament that season. However, Kansas would once again see an early exit from March Madness. Paul Pierce scored 23 points against the ninth-seeded Rhode Island squad.[vi] However, the Jayhawks would lose in just the second round after making it to the Elite Eight in 1996 and the Sweet 16 in 1997.

The loss in the NCAA Tournament once again had Paul Pierce deeply disappointed at how he could not deliver a title despite three excellent regular season records. Though it would have been great if he had stayed one more year to try to win the elusive NCAA championship, Pierce had already decided that he was going to the NBA. He dreamt of winning an NCAA title, but his aspirations of making it to the NBA when he had the best chance to do so was bigger than all of his other aspirations in life. In his announcement, he said that "it was his time" to try his hand at the NBA Draft. Coach Roy Williams, though saddened by the news that he would lose his best player, was still grateful and happy for Pierce and wholeheartedly thanked the rising star for three great years as he gave him his blessing for a good career in the NBA.[vi]

Chapter 4: Paul Pierce's NBA Career

Getting Drafted

Paul Pierce joined a 1998 NBA Draft that seemed like it did not have a lot of talent initially, though it would produce the likes of Dirk Nowitzki, Vince Carter, Baron Davis, Jason Williams, and Antawn Jamison. Due to the initial belief that the talent pool in that draft class was a little weak, Paul Pierce had a great chance of cracking into the top five. If not, then he was certainly a top-10 pick, especially with how he developed in three years with Kansas and how he had continually shown his ability to torch opposing teams.

Pierce came into the draft as a legitimate 6'6" player. He could have even been 6'7" under the right conditions. The small forward out of Kansas also had an NBA-ready body. He was not skinny nor overly muscular, but he was 230 pounds of solid mass.[vii] Thus, he already had the size required to play against veteran small forwards. He could even go down one more position to bully smaller shooting guards with his muscular build.

Many believed that Paul Pierce already had a solid offensive game heading into the NBA. Most of the skills he specialized in were already good enough to be on par with other NBA players that had the same skill sets. Paul had a solid traditional game. He did not do a lot of spectacular or jaw-dropping things on the floor. His game was more suited for the older era of the NBA since he relied mostly on fundamental skills. Pierce was a terrific midrange shooter. He would spot up at that range and immediately hoist up a good-looking jumper. In one-on-one situations, he would dribble once or twice and then pull up from the perimeter.[viii] Paul Pierce also had a dependable shot from beyond the three-point line. He didn't dwell a lot on that shot when he was in college, but when he did, he showed that he could contribute from that range as well.[ix] Idolizing old school guys like Larry Bird and Magic Johnson helped him a lot in developing his fundamental skills.

Pierce's physical attributes were also impressive. He came in already big and strong at his position. That meant that he could bully and post up lankier defenders. If matched up against bigger and stronger opponents, Paul Pierce had a good first step and enough athleticism to blow past slower legs and finish strong at the basket.

The other aspects of Paul Pierce's game were also at steady levels. Pierce could dribble the ball well for his position, though it was still a skill that was in need of more development. He had not shown a knack for passing, but when he did, he could make excellent passes. Pierce could also move without the ball very well as he would find screens and open spots on the floor for good shot attempts. Paul could also defend at a decent level. He had a knack for finding rebounds despite his lack of height and explosive hops. Pierce also improved on defense by leaps and bounds in three years of college. However, his skills were still a work in progress. Nevertheless, he had shown the ability to steal the ball and block shots better than most players at his position.[viii]

Paul Pierce did not have many weaknesses, but the few that he had were glaring. Pierce had the tendency to over-dribble. Because of that, he would often turn the ball over despite having ball-handling abilities that were good enough for the NBA. Pierce had a quick first step and above average handles, however, the reason for him turning the ball over too much was his tendency to get into traffic situations without an idea of how to get out of them. That kind of carelessness and recklessness frequently gave the other team the possession of the ball. His other weakness was his inconsistency on his jump shot. Paul was a hotshot from beyond the arc in his second year in college, but that part of his game devolved in his final year despite the overall increase in his field goal shooting. The reason for that was his tendency of getting in and out of hot streaks from time to time. There were days when his jumper was money, but there were also games where he could not find the mark despite the consistently good form on his jump shot.[viii]

Despite a few glaring weaknesses, Paul Pierce was a surefire top 10 prospect that had the makings of a top five draftee. Paul was a good scorer that relied more on fundamental skills than on terrific, jaw-dropping plays. His basketball IQ was so high coming into the NBA that he would rely more on making the right basic play rather than high-flying finishes at the rim. As such, many scouts believed that Pierce had all the makings of an All-Star because of how well he understood the game and how polished his offensive game was at such a young age.[viiiix]

Draft day came and Paul Pierce was patiently waiting for his name to be called by an NBA team. The first pick belonged to the Los Angeles Clippers. Pierce would have loved to be drafted by the Clippers because of how close to home LA was. However, the Clips went on to choose center Michael Olowokandi, who would never develop into a good NBA player. Olowokandi would eventually become one of the biggest draft busts in league history. In the next few selections, teams were not wrong in recruiting the likes of Mike Bibby, Antawn Jamison, Vince Carter, Jason Williams, and Larry Hughes. All of those players would have good NBA careers, though they were never as good as Pierce was in his prime. However, nine teams passed on drafting Pierce to the surprise of a lot of analysts and Paul himself.

Pierce was surprised that none of the top teams in the draft picked him. He had worked out for four different teams that had a place in the top five of the NBA Draft. They had promised to draft him if he was available, but somehow, they never did. Even the Philadelphia 76ers, who had the eighth pick in the draft, had a good chance of pairing Allen Iverson with a future Hall of Famer. However, they chose to select Larry Hughes instead. In an interview conducted in February 2016, Paul Pierce would say that the Sixers had missed the chance to form what would have been one of the deadliest duos in NBA history. Pierce would even say he and A.I. would have been multiple-time champions had the Sixers drafted him.[x]

For Paul Pierce's part, he believed that his fall in the draft board was because of his lack of explosive athleticism. He thought that a lot of NBA teams rated players based on their raw outputs: their size, length, athleticism, and speed. Most NBA teams, especially now, do not give a lot of premium to fundamental skills and basketball IQ, which were both the calling cards of Paul Pierce. As he reminisced on how far he fell when he joined the NBA Draft in 1998, Paul Pierce would even say in a recent interview that he probably would not have been drafted today based on his profile in 1998.[xi]

The next pick, the ninth one, belonged to the Milwaukee Bucks, who were goaded by the Dallas Mavericks into picking the little-known German 7-footer, Dirk Nowitzki. The Mavs would pull off a great draft move that had the Bucks moving Dirk to Dallas in exchange for a few role players and the sixth pick in that year's draft. The Mavs were not wrong in that decision as they knew what Dirk Nowitzki could do. Dirk would develop into arguably the best international player in NBA history.

The Boston Celtics, who had the 10th pick in the draft, were next. The Celtics had originally planned on drafting Dirk Nowitzki, who only worked out for a few teams. Because of how relatively unknown Dirk was to other teams, Boston believed that they would surely be able to draft the German. The Celtics envisioned making Dirk the next coming of Larry Bird. However, the Mavericks were also interested in Nowitzki after seeing him in a workout. They knew that Boston would surely draft him with the 10th pick. Hence, they pulled off a move that stole Dirk Nowitzki away from the Celtic franchise.

With their plans foiled, the Boston Celtics proceeded to plan B, which was to take the best available player. Then-Boston Celtics coach Rick Pitino was shocked that Paul Pierce's name was still available on the board. He knew how good the Kansas product was, but was still in amazement that no team decided to take him. He then heard rumors concerning why. Then-Denver Nuggets general manager Dan Issel had thought that Paul Pierce was a very soft player. Because of that, the Nuggets decided to take Pierce's college teammate Raef LaFrentz, who never blossomed into an All-Star in the NBA. That "soft" tag might have also turned off other NBA teams.[xii]

But Pitino thought something was wrong. The Celtics called up Roy Williams of Kansas to inquire about Pierce's health. Williams assured Pitino that Pierce was completely healthy. Because of that, the Celtics did not hesitate to draft Paul Pierce.[xii] Paul was a player they did not even think of as part of their plan because they thought that he would already be taken way ahead of the 10th pick. Then-Celtics general manager Chris Wallace would go on to say that they never had plans of getting Pierce unless he was available.[v] Though their original plan of taking Dirk Nowitzki did not turn out as they expected, it did not hurt that they were able to secure the services of Paul Pierce, whose career turned out to be on par with that of Dirk's. And more than that, Paul Pierce was about to become the Boston Celtics' franchise player.

Pierce, for his part, was also in a little bit of disbelief. He was shocked at how he ended up getting drafted 10th. He was also shocked at how he was drafted by the Boston Celtics, the very same team that made it hard for his hometown team the Los Angeles Lakers to dominate during the 80's. It was a difficult pill for Paul to swallow knowing that he would be spending the next few years as a Celtic. Nevertheless, the most important thing was that he was in the NBA. He was happy with how far he had made it as an aspiring professional basketball player.

Rookie Season

Coming into the lockout-shortened 50-game season during the 1998-99 NBA year, Paul Pierce was a favorite for the Rookie of the Year award because of how many people thought he could produce right away with the scoring abilities he had compared to the other rookies, who were more or less raw compared to him. But Paul, on his part, also had a lot of expectations on his shoulders. He was set to play for the Boston Celtics, the winningest franchise as far as championships went in the history of the NBA. He was ready to carry the burden that used to fall on the shoulders of legendary players such as Bill Russell, John Havlicek, Larry Bird, and Kevin McHale.

But Paul would not disappoint the Celtics team that had been desperately searching for a new franchise player ever since the retirement of Larry Bird earlier in the decade. Similar to his college career, Paul Pierce was immediately a starter from the get-go of his NBA years. Despite that, he was not yet the best player as he had to develop into one while earning the trust of the team and the franchise on the way.

In his very first game as an NBA player, Paul Pierce delivered 19 points, nine rebounds, and five assists on 50% shooting from both the floor and the three-point arc. He was matched up with Toronto's high-flying rookie Vince Carter in that 11-point loss on February 5, 1999. In the next game, Pierce finally delivered a win for Boston, posting 19 points on 10 out of 12 shooting from the foul line against the Cleveland Cavaliers. Even as early as his first two games, Paul Pierce was already showing flashes of what he could do as a scorer. He was not scoring well because Boston lacked capable players. He was playing alongside Antoine Walker and several capable scorers, but he was still able to produce right away.

After scoring back-to-back 19-point games in his fourth and fifth games, Paul Pierce would break the 20-point mark on February 17. He had 26 points, seven rebounds, and a then-career high seven steals. In that overtime win against the Vancouver Grizzlies, Paul shot 9 out of 21 from the field in 49 minutes of action. On February 21, Paul Pierce would have his first 20-10 double-double rebound game. He had 24 points and 12 rebounds in a loss to the Washington Wizards. That was the third of a three-game streak of scoring at least 20 points for the talented rookie named Paul Pierce. Though Paul Pierce had a good start in his NBA career by scoring in double digits in his first 12 games, it appeared that the rookie still had a lot to learn as he adjusted to the big leagues.

Pierce would find himself struggling for the majority of March that season. He had eight games of scoring in single digits for the whole month compared to how he was a high double-digit scorer for the month of February. However, Pierce would bounce back in April. He would find his scoring touch again as he constantly scored more than 20 points in that month. Paul Pierce had 23 points on 4 out of 5 shooting from beyond the arc in a loss to the Orlando Magic on April 5. He also had six rebounds, four assists, and four steals in that game. In their next game versus the Washington Wizards, Paul would once again score 23 points in a 21-point blowout win. He would then have a then-career high of 13 rebounds versus the Sixers in a loss.

On April 18, Paul Pierce would establish a new career high. He had 26 points on 9 out of 15 shooting from the field in a win versus the Wizards. Paul also finished with seven rebounds and five steals in that game. In the very next game, the budding star would deliver his best individual performance as an NBA professional at that time. He had 30 points, 12 rebounds, and six dimes in a loss to the Indiana Pacers. Those 30 points were a new career high for him.

Paul Pierce would round up his rookie season with good individual performances coupled with big wins. On April 23 and 25, the Boston Celtics won consecutive games by 29 points each. Pierce combined for 29 points in both games and was efficient in helping the team win those games. A few nights later, Paul Pierce would score a new career high of 31 points on the Miami Heat. He made 12 out of 19 shots from the floor and 3 out of 6 from downtown in that game. The Celtics won that game by 11 points. Paul Pierce ended his rookie season with 27 points, 9 rebounds, and 5 assists in a loss to the Charlotte Hornets.

At the end of his first campaign as an NBA player, Paul Pierce averaged 16.5 points, 6.4 rebounds, 2.4 assists, and 1.7 steals in 34 minutes of action. Pierce finished behind Antoine Walker and Ron Mercer for the team's scoring leadership that season. He started all but one of the games he played in while shooting 44% from the field and 41.2% from beyond the arc. He was a member of the All-Rookie First Team, but lost out to Vince Carter for the Rookie of the Year Award as the rookie of Toronto wowed fans with his high-flying abilities and scoring explosions. It also did not help Paul Pierce that the Celtics finished the season with a sub-par record of 19-31. Other than some high-scoring games for the rookie, Paul Pierce did not have a lot of highlights that season, especially because of how badly his team was playing.

The Rising Franchise Player

Though the Boston Celtics did not enjoy a particularly good year of basketball in the 1998-99 season, their bright spot was Paul Pierce, who had all the potential to make it big in the NBA. They were not wrong in drafting the former Kansas Jayhawk with the 10th overall pick. As for the teams that did not draft Nowitzki, Carter, or Pierce, they must have been quite upset for passing up on a young man that would have done wonders for their franchise immediately.

It was during Paul Pierce's second season in the NBA that he began to show fans and analysts what he could do as a franchise player in the future. The Boston fan base warmed up quickly to the emotional character and physicality of the fast-developing small forward. For his part, Paul Pierce was also quick to adjust to the different style of the NBA. The NBA game was physical, and so was Paul Pierce. The NBA game was emotionally taxing, but Pierce was emotionally strong. He was simply a man that was perfect for the NBA style.

In his first game in his second season in the NBA, Paul Pierce had 30 points, eight rebounds, and five assists as he led the Celtics to a win over the Toronto Raptors in a matchup between the previous season's two best rookies. Pierce would have his first double-double game of the season when he delivered 30 points, 11 rebounds, four assists, and four steals in an 11-point win versus the Cleveland Cavaliers on November 17. He would have his second double-double performance when he had 17 points and 12 rebounds in a 10-point win versus the Indiana Pacers on November 22. Pierce then scored 22 points on November 26 as Pierce started his second season scoring in double digits throughout his first 13 games.

In a 12-point win versus the Miami Heat on December 3, Paul Pierce delivered 26 points, five rebounds, four assists, and a career-high nine steals. He was quickly showing that he was not only a capable offensive scorer, but also a dependable defensive gem, especially when it came to stealing possessions. When other people thought that Pierce was merely a high scorer, he put on a show at the defensive end as he proved that he was also one of the best defenders when he was young. Paul would, however, miss a few games shortly after that win because of an injury. Pierce made his return on December 26 against the LA Clippers, the second team of his hometown. In that loss, Paul Pierce had 24 points, six rebounds, and seven assists while making 11 of 12 free throws.

On January 17, Paul Pierce would explode for his new career high of 34 points in a win against the Washington Wizards. He also had five steals in that game as he managed to play in the most efficient way. Pierce shot 12 out of 16 from the field and 10 out of 10 from the foul line in that win. Two nights later, the Celtics would win again as Pierce went for his first back-to-back 30-point games. He had 30 points, seven rebounds, four steals, and three blocks in that win. Pierce and the Celtics rounded up a three-game streak as the rising small forward had 21 points, ten rebounds, and four steals in a 25-point win versus the Seattle SuperSonics on January 21. What that meant for Pierce was that he was not only a growing star as far as the individual level was concerned, but was also budding into a player that could lead a team with solid performances.

On February 8, he almost had his first career triple-double as he recorded 17 points, 11 rebounds, and nine assists in a loss to the New Jersey Nets. He was quickly rounding himself into a solid all-around player when everyone thought that he was merely a scorer. Paul Pierce would take part in the Rising Stars Challenge at the All-Star Weekend that year. He was not able to participate in that event during his rookie season since the All-Star Weekend was suspended due to the lockout. He played for the Sophomore Team that lost to the Rookie Squad that season. Even so, Paul Pierce led all second-year players with 18 points on 5 out of 11 shooting from beyond the arc.

A few weeks after the midseason break, Pierce would then go back-to-back against the two other great rookies of the 1998 draft class. He first scored 21 points in a loss to Dirk Nowitzki and the Dallas Mavericks before putting up 22 points in a battle versus Vince Carter and the Toronto Raptors on March 1. The Celtics would then go to Toronto to go up against the Raptors in back-to-back games. Pierce would only score 11 in that fourth straight loss. With those performances, there was no doubt that

Pierce could have been drafted higher than both Dirk and Vince as he displayed his star prowess against the two future Hall-of-Famers.

On March 12, the rising forward scored a new career high of 38 points together with seven rebounds and four steals in a losing effort against the Philadelphia 76ers. He made 11 of 15 field-goal attempts, 4 of 5 three-point shots, and 12 of 17 free-throw attempts. On March 24, Paul Pierce would go for at least 30 points again as he scored 31 points together with eight rebounds in a loss to the Sixers. Later on, the Celtics found themselves in a 10-game losing streak. Though the Celtics, at that point, were already well out of playoff contention, Boston won five of their next six games to end the season. Pierce did not attempt to shoot a lot of field goals in all six games as he opted to incorporate his teammates to improve team chemistry for the next season.

In his second year in the NBA, Paul Pierced improved with averages of 19.5 points, 5.4 rebounds, 3 assists, and 2.1 steals while shooting 44.2% from the floor. Despite a marked improvement from their future franchise superstar, the Boston Celtics were merely 35-47 throughout the season. They missed the playoffs yet again despite having a stronger lineup. However, the bright side to all of that was that the Celtics were a vastly improved team, especially with an improving Paul Pierce leading the charge for Boston's future in basketball.

Breakout Season

After a much-improved personal season for Paul Pierce in 1999-2000, he knew he was ready to break out of his shell to become a legitimate star in the NBA by the time his third season in the league started. He would go on to say that he was ready to show the world what he had as a player and that he was prepared to unleash the beast inside of him. The dragon was ready to be unleashed, as Paul Pierce would say.[iv] As we know, Pierce was true to his word as he began to score at a career-high rate in the 2000-01 season.

Paul Pierce's breakout season, his whole NBA career, and even his life almost went down the drain because of a horrific incident in September of 2000 before the season started. Paul Pierce and a few of his teammates had decided to party at a club called the Buzz Club. Paul Pierce went to mingle with some ladies when things suddenly got heated between himself and a few other men. Before Pierce knew it, he had suddenly become the victim of a stabbing. He had received 11 stab wounds all around his body. At that moment, the world was almost robbed of what would become one of the most thrilling basketball players of the era. [xiii]

Boston police swiftly responded to the incident in the middle of the night. Paul Pierce was rushed by a teammate, Tony Battie, to the hospital which was just a few minutes away from the nightclub. That was one of the few factors that saved Paul Pierce from certain death. Luckily, he was also wearing a thick leather jacket that prevented the knife from getting anywhere near his vital organs.[iv] Paul Pierce was saved from the incident and would recover in time for the upcoming NBA season.

Paul Pierce was a little thankful about the incident afterwards. He said that this near-death experience forced him to mature tenfold. He learned how to appreciate life for what it is because he almost lost his own. Paul Pierce would pour all of his focus into basketball instead of spending time doing the activities that led to his near-death experience. This was a more mature Paul Pierce coming into the new season. His sudden maturity was vital for his sudden breakout in the 2000-01 season.[iv]

Just a month after the stabbing incident, Paul Pierce was completely healthy and ready to go for another 82-game grind in the NBA. In his first game of the season, he had 28 points, six rebounds, and five assists in a 20-point win versus the

Detroit Pistons. In the very next game, he went for 30 points in a tight win against the Toronto Raptors. It did not seem like he had just recovered from multiple stab injuries just about a month before those performances. Paul Pierce almost seemed superhuman with how quick he recovered and got back to prime basketball form.

In a game against the Orlando Magic on November 24, Paul Pierce showed that he was indeed a rising star in the NBA as he scored 41 points in an overtime win against the Magic. In that new career-high game, he was 13 out of 22 from the floor and 12 out of 17 from the foul stripe. From that point on, there was no stopping Paul Pierce on his way to NBA stardom. The man was on a mission to become one of the greatest. Nothing could derail his confidence after that explosion versus the Magic. Despite some superhuman efforts from Paul Pierce, a few losses and struggles showed that he was still a mortal man. He was 0 of 7 from the field and scored 9 points from the free throw line. He was then limited to mediocre scoring outputs in the next two games, which were both losses.

After that losing stretch, the Boston Celtics found themselves back in the winning column for just a few moments. The Celtics defeated the New Jersey Nets on December 20 by 13 points before visiting the Knicks to win by six. Pierce had 25 versus the Nets as he hit 13 free throws before he scorched New York for 31 points on 13 out of 21 from the field. Pierce would have 28 points and seven rebounds in their next game versus the Bucks, but they ended up losing that game by five.

Paul Pierce recorded a new career high versus the Minnesota Timberwolves on January 15, 2001. He shot 15 out of 22 from the field and 11 out of 12 from the free throw line to reach 42 points in a five-point win against the Wolves and Kevin Garnett, who would later become one of his best friends and teammates. In the fifth game of a six-game scoring run, Paul Pierce went for 40 points and 7 rebounds against the Detroit Pistons just a few days after he scored 28 on them. He was 14 out of 19 from the field and 5 out of 7 from beyond the arc in that game. That was the third time he broke the 40-point barrier that season. It would not be the last time as Pierce's great performances were not mere flukes.

On February 5, Pierce made a strong claim for an All-Star spot that year as he went for 39 points on 12 of 21 shooting from the field and 13 out of 16 from the foul stripe. However, the Celtics ended up losing that game by 12 points to the Toronto Raptors. Despite a strong case and a mighty showing the entire season, Paul Pierce was not selected as an All-Star for the Eastern Conference squad. He arguably deserved a spot in that midseason classic as he was playing a lot better than three other small forwards that made the cut. Pierce was scoring and rebounding a lot more than the Knicks' Latrell Sprewell. He was also averaging more points than the Bucks' Glenn Robinson. Paul was even more deserving than Grant Hill, who was voted in the All-Star Game as a starter despite playing merely four games the entire season. It was a travesty that Paul Pierce, who was averaging about 25 points, was not selected by the coaches to play in the All-Star Game.

Despite the apparent snub of Paul Pierce in the annual All-Star Game, he went back to work to help the Boston Celtics get back to NBA relevance. March 13 was when The Truth was truly and finally out. Paul Pierce went back to his hometown of Los Angeles to score 42 big points against the team he had watched and idolized as a young boy. He made 13 of 19 field goals and 3 of 7 three-point attempts. The chink in his armor during that game was that he struggled from the foul line, only going for 13 of 21. Had he made more, the Celtics would have won the game as the Lakers would only win by five. Paul was so skilled that Lakers center Shaquille O'Neal went on to commend him in the post-game interview by calling him "The Truth".[i] Shaq was so impressed that he gave Pierce a nickname. The name would stick to Pierce after that. Just two nights after his historic 42-

point performance in Los Angeles, Paul Pierce went to Phoenix to torch the Suns with another 42-point game. He made 13 of 25 field goal attempts while shooting 3 of 8 three-pointers and 13 of 13 free throws.

On March 22, Paul Pierce had a new career high, which was the third time he had re-established a new career high that season. In a 15-point win versus the New Jersey Nets, he scored 44 points as he shot 15 of 26 from the field, 4 of 9 from downtown, and 10 out of 10 from the foul stripe. But Pierce was not done yet. Three days after that career game, he went on to score 36 points on the Chicago Bulls. He made 11 of 21 field goals and 11 of 14 free throws. Right after that match, he then had 41 points and 11 rebounds in a win over the Atlanta Hawks. That game rounded up what was Pierce's best four-game stretch of the season. The Celtics were 3-1 in that stretch. On April 11, Pierce would have his eighth game of scoring at least 40 points. He had 41 in a loss to the Heat and made 12 of 23 field goal attempts and 15 of 16 free throw shots.

By the end of the 2000-01 regular season, Paul Pierce averaged a then-career high of 25.3 points together with 6.4 rebounds, 3.1 assists, and 1.7 steals while shooting 45.4% from the floor and 38% from the three-point line in 38 minutes of action. Amazingly, Pierce played all 82 games of the season even after getting stabbed about a month before the regular season started. He was the Celtics' leading scorer that year. Despite a career year for the breakout star of the Boston Celtics, the Green Team would only win 36 of their 82 games that season. Pierce would miss the playoffs for the third straight season since being drafted.

First All-Star Season, First Playoff Appearance, Breaking Through to the Eastern Conference Finals

After several seasons of failing to reach the playoffs, the Boston Celtics permanently replaced Rick Pitino with Jim O'Brien who would begin to start a new culture with the Boston Celtics. Because of the new coach and system, the Celtics were not on anyone's list of playoff-bound teams. During the regular season, they would prove the league wrong. And despite the new coach, Paul Pierce showed that his star-caliber game was universal to any system as he flourished even more under O'Brien.

Paul Pierce started the new season scoring off well by scoring 29 points in only 28 minutes in a win over the Cleveland Cavaliers. The very next night, Pierce went for 36 points and ten rebounds in a narrow loss to the New Jersey Nets. He would go for 35 points in a win versus the Seattle SuperSonics on November 9, 2001. He made 13 of 26 field goal attempts and a fantastic 8 out of 12 three-point shots in that game.

The Boston Celtics would find themselves on the winning track starting November 27. Pierce had several spectacular games in what turned into a six-game winning streak. He first scored 33 points in 31 minutes as the Celtics won by merely a point versus the Miami Heat. On December 1, Pierce would establish as new career high versus the New Jersey Nets. Paul Pierce had 48 points and 12 rebounds in an overtime win against the Nets. He went 13 of 34 from the field, 5 out of 8 from the three-point arc, and 17 of 18 from the foul line.

December 14, Paul would have 38 points, 12 rebounds, five assists, and four steals in a win versus the Chicago Bulls. He made 50% of his shots that game. Pierce would follow that performance with another double-double as he put up 30 points and ten rebounds against the Charlotte Hornets. In a win against the Utah Jazz on December 21, he put up 36 points on 10 of 22 shooting from the field. In the game before that, he had five big blocks against the Cleveland Cavaliers. Paul Pierce was suddenly beginning to do it all for the Boston Celtics, who were winning at a rate they had not seen in a very long time.

In an overtime game against the Clippers, Paul Pierce wowed his hometown crowd of Los Angeles by recording 35 points, ten rebounds, and six assists as he led the Celtics to victory despite a 10 of 32 shooting night from Boston's rising superstar. Because of his steady play throughout the season as a dominant force in all facets of the game, Paul Pierce was selected to play in his first All-Star Game for the Eastern Conference squad. He almost got snubbed again, only barely coming in as the final selection by the coaches.

On February 19, Pierce would have 33 points, eight rebounds, and five steals in a win versus their rivals the Los Angeles Lakers. Pierce was 12 of 21 from the field in that classic game. On February 23, he went for five steals again in a loss to the Houston Rockets. On March 11, Pierce went for 37 big points in a win against the Washington Wizards. He made 15 of his 23 attempts from the field and 5 of his nine shots from beyond the arc. Pierce would not stop scoring big that season as he continued to contribute more high-scoring games in the Celtics' quest to get back to the playoffs.

By the end of the 2001-02 season, Paul Pierce averaged new career highs of 26.1 points, 6.9 rebounds, and 3.2 assists in 40.3 minutes of action. He shot 44.2% from the floor and 40.4% from the three-point line as he began shooting more three-pointers under O'Brien's system. Despite shooting more three-pointers, Pierce was making a then career-high of 80.2% of his foul shots. Not only did Pierce lead the Celtics in scoring, he was also the overall leader in total points in the NBA that season as he played all 82 games. Because of that, Paul Pierce was voted into the All-NBA Third Team for the very first time. There was no doubt that Paul Pierce had grown to a legitimate superstar after only four years of playing in the NBA. His team was rising with him as well; the Boston Celtics made the playoffs for the first time since the mid-90's with a record of 49-33. They were the third seed in the Eastern Conference. Paul Pierce was heading towards his first playoff appearance.

In the first round of the 2002 playoffs, Paul Pierce and the Celtics went head-to-head with the Philadelphia 76ers, who went all the way to the NBA Finals the season before. It was going to be a battle between Pierce and Allen Iverson, who were two of the best scorers in the NBA that season. Flashback to 1998 when the Philadelphia 76ers had the chance to form a deadly duo of Allen Iverson and Paul Pierce, had they chosen to draft the latter with the eighth overall pick. Instead, they selected Larry Hughes, who had a respectable career as a scorer, but he would not develop into the kind of player that Pierce became. Now, the Sixers had to face the scoring prowess of

Paul Pierce in the first round. They would regret having chosen Hughes over Pierce because the latter would torch them in that series.

In Game 1 of that series, Paul Pierce got the better of Allen Iverson. He had 31 points, 11 rebounds, four steals, and three blocks. Meanwhile, A.I. was limited to merely 20 points on a miserable shooting night. The Celtics also defeated the 76ers by 10 points. Pierce and company would not let up in Game 2 as they showed why they deserved to be in the playoffs after seven years of missing the postseason tournament. The Truth went for another double-double game as he scored 25 points and grabbed ten rebounds. Boston won by eight points in that match.

Paul Pierce had his third straight double-double performance in Game 3 as he did not show any jitters in his first three playoff games. He had 29 points, ten rebounds, and seven assists. Pierce made 8 of his 20 field goal attempts which included five from beyond the arc. However, Allen Iverson exploded for 42 big points to lead the Sixers to a five-point win and to inch within a game closer to the Celtics' lead. The Philadelphia 76ers would complete their quest to tie the series up as they won Game 4 by merely two points. Pierce had 20 points, which was his lowest for the entire series.

Paul Pierce would not let the 76ers take the series win. In Game 5, he singlehandedly destroyed the whole Philadelphia squad as he went for a then playoff career high of 46 big points. Pierce made 16 of his 25 field goal attempts as well as 8 of his ten shots from beyond the arc in that win. More importantly, the Boston Celtics defeated the Sixers by 33 points. With that win, the Boston Celtics secured a berth in the second round of that year's edition of the NBA playoffs. They would meet the ever-improving Detroit Pistons.

In Game 1 of the second-round series against the Pistons, Paul Pierce went for his fourth double-double of the playoffs. He had 17 points and ten rebounds to go with five assists and three steals. However, Detroit took that game by 12 points as the Pistons' defense proved to be tougher than the Sixers'. In Game 2, the Celtics would end up taking home court advantage away from their opponents. Pierce was instrumental and assisted them in the win by scoring 22 points and grabbing six rebounds.

As the series shifted over to Boston for Games 3 and 4, the Celtics showed how important that Game 2 win was. They would win the first game of their home battle by merely two points. Paul Pierce contributed with 19 points, five rebounds, and five assists though he struggled from the floor with a 30% shooting clip. However, The Truth was a difficult pill for the

Detroit Pistons to swallow in Game 4, which saw Paul Pierce going for 25 points and an incredible playoff career high of 17 rebounds to go along with six assists and three blocks. The Celtics fended the Pistons off in that game by 11 points. Pierce and company would bury the Detroit Pistons in Game 5, quickly sweeping Games 2 onwards after losing the first outing. In only 31 minutes, Paul Pierce delivered 18 points and five rebounds as Boston won the game by nine points. With that win, the Celtics had a chance to get back to the NBA Finals for the first time since the days of Larry Bird by winning the Eastern Conference championship.

In Boston Celtics' way were the top-seeded New Jersey Nets, who were led by All-Star all-around point guard Jason Kidd. In Game 1 of that series, Paul Pierce went for 27 points on 9 out of 19 shooting from the field. However, the Nets drew first blood by winning that game by seven points. The Celtics bounced back in Game 2 by taking home court advantage, which was similar to what they did with the Detroit Pistons. They won that game by seven points. Pierce was instrumental in that game despite having a mediocre scoring output. He had 18 points an a measly 3 out of 20 shooting clip from the floor and 11 out of 20 from the foul line, but grabbed 14 crucial rebounds.

In Game 3 of that series, Paul Pierce showed why he was a big shot maker in big time games. The Celtics found themselves in a 21-point deficit entering the fourth quarter. For any team, it was easy for them just to call it a loss and move on to the next game. However, not every team had The Truth. Throughout the first three quarters of play, Paul Pierce was limited to merely 9 points. However, he was the key to the enormous fourth quarter comeback. He scored 19 points in those final 12 minutes and led the Celtics to one of the most memorable come-from-behind wins in NBA lore. He finished with 28 points as the Celtics took a 2-1 advantage and sought to repeat what they did to the Detroit Pistons.

Paul Pierce headed off to score 31 points and grabbed nine rebounds in Game 4 for the Boston Celtics who were looking to protect home court. However, the Nets were also clutch in their own right and defeated Boston by merely two points. Pierce came back to New Jersey to score 24 points and collect 12 rebounds in 43 minutes of action. However, the Nets made sure they held on to their big lead to win the game by 11. With the series on the line, Paul Pierce would struggle in Game 6, shooting only 5 of 16 from the field to score 14 points, his lowest the entire playoffs. Because their star player could not deliver in that crucial moment, the Celtics ended up losing to the Nets in six games. Despite the loss, Paul Pierce and his teammates had no reason to be disappointed because they had made it deeper into the postseason than anyone had expected.

Falling Short Again

Having tasted what it was like to contend for a chance at an NBA championship, Paul Pierce would not allow himself or his team to go back to the mediocre days of the Celtics franchise. He wanted the taste of playoff victories, and he wanted to remain in contention for the NBA title for several more years to come. Paul Pierce made sure that he was playing at the highest level possible to help his team maintain their status as perennial playoff contenders.

In his first game of the 2002-03 season, Paul Pierce had 28 points, seven rebounds, and seven assists. He made 11 of his 22 field goal attempts in 40 minutes of action in that loss to the Chicago Bulls. In the Celtics' next game, Pierce was limited to 3 out of 16 shooting from the field for only 12 points. Boston lost that game to Washington by an embarrassing 45 points. Embarrassed about his performance in his last game, Paul Pierce went to New York on November 2, 2002, to score 46 big points on the Knicks. In that victory, Pierce was 12 of 22 from the floor and 20 out of 21 from the charity stripe. From then on, the Boston Celtics went on a six-game run after opening the season with two straight losses.

On December 2, Pierce narrowly missed the opportunity to record his first career triple-double when he had 27 points, ten rebounds, and eight assists in a win over the Orlando Magic. On December 20, he achieved his first game of scoring more than 40 points with 42 points, 14 rebounds, and 4 steals against the Minnesota Timberwolves in a nine-point win.

After being limited to 15 points in a win versus Milwaukee sometime in January 2003, Pierce went for 40 points, seven rebounds, six assists, and four steals in a one-point win over the Philadelphia 76ers on January 20. Just four days after he scored 40 points, Paul Pierce had 45 points and ten rebounds in a 19-point win against the Denver Nuggets. He was 16 out of 27 from the field, 4 of 7 from the three-point line, and 9 out of 10 from the charity stripe. On January 26, Paul Pierce finally compiled his first career triple-double after five years in the NBA. He had 27 points, 13 rebounds, and 13 assists in a 45-minute performance against the Orlando Magic. The Boston Celtics, however, lost by 52 points to the Detroit Pistons on January 31. Pierce had 23 points in that embarrassing loss.

Five days after the historic loss, Paul Pierce and his Celtics sent the Seattle SuperSonics packing by defeating them by 40 points. Pierce contributed with 26 points, eight rebounds, and six dimes in that big win. Because of his steady performance as the Boston Celtics' sole superstar, Paul Pierce was selected to play in his second All-Star Game that season. The superstar small forward proved that he was not just a one-trick pony by making it to the All-Star team in back-to-back seasons. Paul Pierce was a steady scorer up until the end of the regular season. On April 4, he had another 40-point game, making 12 of his 23 field goal attempts and 13 of his 18 free throw shots against the Sacramento Kings in a narrow loss.

At the end of his second All-Star season, Paul Pierce averaged 25.9 points, 7.3 rebounds, 4.4 assists, and 1.8 steals. He made the All-NBA Third Team that season for the second time. He became a better rebounder and playmaker, and was molding into a complete all-around player for the Boston Celtics after several years of being merely a scorer. In that season, Pierce's field goal shooting dropped to 41.6%, but the Celtics were still winning games with a record of 44 wins as against 38 losses. They came into the playoffs as the sixth seed.

Paul Pierce would start the first round of the playoffs with a bang. Against the Indiana Pacers, Pierce delivered 40 points, 11 rebounds, six assists, and four steals in a Game 1 victory. However, he was limited to 12 points as Indiana took Game 2. When the Celtics went home to Boston for the next two games, Pierce had 21 points and 12 rebounds in an 18-point win in Game 3 before putting up 37 points, ten rebounds, and seven assists as they took a 3-1 advantage after Game 4. Indiana would push the series to at least one more game by winning Game 5. In Game 6, The Truth and the Celtics were unstoppable for the Pacers as the Green Team won the series thanks to the 27 points of Paul Pierce.

In the second round of the postseason, the Boston Celtics would get a chance to redeem their loss in the Eastern Conference Finals of 2002, this time by defeating the New Jersey Nets. However, things did not turn out the way they had planned. In Game 1, Pierce delivered 34 points and eight assists, but the Nets won by four points. In Game 2, The Truth had his first playoff and career triple-double when he posted 32 points, ten rebounds, and 11 assists. However, New Jersey still took that one. Pierce would then post 23 points and ten boards in Game 3, but they lost that one by 18 big points. No team in NBA history has ever come back to win from a 0-3 deficit in a seven-game series. It was only a matter of time before the Celtics would become a part of a historical statistic. It turned out that the end came more quickly than they wanted it to as the Nets won Game 4 in overtime. Pierce had 27 points, ten rebounds, and seven assists in that loss. Despite good numbers from Paul Pierce in that four-game sweep, it was clear that the Boston Celtics were relying too much on their lone superstar.

Transition Period

The Boston Celtics were in for significant changes for the 2003-04 season. Firstly, the franchise hired Danny Ainge, who was a former guard for the Celtics during their championship years, as the new general manager. Ainge made a couple of decisions to shake the team up. He first sent Antoine Walker, the team's second-leading scorer and Pierce's reliever on offense, to the Dallas Mavericks in exchange for Pierce's former college teammate Raef LaFrentz and several other role players. The decision was made because Ainge believed that the Celtics were going nowhere with the duo of Pierce and Walker.

With the change in the lineup, Paul Pierce would come into the 2003-04 season as the sole scoring option of the Boston Celtics. As such, defenses would key on him every single time they could. Nevertheless, Pierce was still productive on offense. He had 23 points in his first game of the season, which was a Celtics win versus Miami by 23 points. He then had 23 again as they defeated Memphis in their next game. After that, however, Pierce would fall into a slump of poor shooting nights. And even when he would score a lot of points, they were in losing efforts, for example when he scored 33 points in a loss to the 76ers on November 21, 2003.

Despite the slow start to the season for Pierce and his team, they still performed well in a few mentionable games. On November 26, Pierce had 30 points on 12 of 22 shooting from the field to lead his Celtics to victory against the Orlando Magic. After that game, he went for his second career regular season triple-double when he recorded 26 points, ten rebounds, and ten assists in a 10-point win versus the Milwaukee Bucks. On December 7, Pierce and Boston broke a four-game streak by winning against the Denver Nuggets. The Truth had 33 points, seven rebounds, and ten assists in that game. The Celtics started winning games after that.

On December 10, Pierce had 36 points and 14 rebounds while contributing with four blocks on the defensive end in a 14-point win against the Seattle SuperSonics. In the next game, he had 33 points and 11 rebounds in a win over the Toronto Raptors. Pierce finished that winning streak and a three-game stretch of high scoring by putting up 41 points, nine rebounds, six assists, and four steals as he matched up with teenage rookie phenom LeBron James.

On December 26, Pierce would dish out 11 dimes in a win over the Phoenix Suns as he displayed an unheralded facet of his game. However, Paul Pierce would find himself in mediocre performances until the end of the calendar year. He would struggle from the floor despite the number of minutes he was playing. It was probably because of how other team's defenses were focused on him since there were no other capable scorers in the Celtic lineup that season. That was when Pierce finally realized that he had become a one-man player. He was the classic example of a great player playing for a mediocre team.

On January 7, 2004, he nearly had another triple-double against the Orlando Magic as he put up 19 points, ten rebounds, and nine assists in a win. He was even nearing a quadruple-double on the wrong side as he had nine turnovers that game. Those turnovers showed that Pierce was merely human as he tried to carry the Celtics on his back by constantly having possession of the ball. Pierce would then put up 30 points, 12 rebounds, and eight assists as he continued to teach the rookie version of LeBron James some lessons in that blowout win versus the Cleveland Cavaliers.

However, it had become a trend for Pierce to find himself in shooting slumps in consecutive games that season. He was limited to merely 4 points on 1 out of 10 shooting from the field in a loss to the Houston Rockets on January 14. The Celtics were not doing so well either. They only won six of their 16 games in the month of January while Pierce was playing. From the end of the month until early February, they were even in a six-game losing stretch.

The Celtics were only able to break out of their slump by winning against the Philadelphia 76ers on February 7 by 30 points. In that game, Pierce would score 35 points on 10 out of 18 shooting from the floor and 13 out of 15 attempts from the charity stripe. He would then score 32 in the next game, which was a loss. On February 12, Pierce was limited to 4 points in a big loss to the Bulls. Despite the many shooting slumps and the continuous skid that the Celtics found themselves in, Paul Pierce was still a superstar and was voted into the All-Star squad of the Eastern Conference. That selection recognized his efforts for leading a mediocre team. Other players who were playing on bad teams would not have made the All-Star team despite terrific numbers posted night in and night out. The reason Pierce was different was because his skills and prowess were palpable even though his team was struggling.

After the All-Star break, the Celtics' fortunes did not improve, instead they went on a seven-game losing streak. Things did not improve any further when Jim O'Brien suddenly stepped down as head coach with the reasoning that he did not see eye-to-eye with Danny Ainge, especially when the latter traded away some of O'Brien's favorite players. Assistant John Carroll took over on an interim basis. Despite the setbacks, Paul Pierce had a few good games in between those losses. He had 27 points against the Kings. The Truth then delivered 34 points, seven rebounds, and six assists in an embarrassing 21-point loss to Seattle.

Despite the losses and disappointments that the Celtics were facing that season, Pierce still tried his best to right the direction of a sinking ship. He had 37 points and 12 rebounds in a win against the Wizards on March 13. After that game, he had 28 points, 11 rebounds, and seven assists in a win against the Nuggets. On March 26, he put up 34 points and eight boards versus the New Jersey Nets in a victory. He then had 32 points in a win over the Warriors on April 2. As the season was winding down, Pierce scored 31 points in a loss to the Miami Heat.

At the end of the season, Pierce averaged 23 points, 6.5 rebounds, and 5.1 assists. He shot merely 40.2% from the floor and struggled to score against the tough defense that was played on the lone star of the Boston Celtics. Despite a drop in his scoring productivity, Paul Pierce managed to make his teammates look better overall as he focused on making plays. His assist numbers that season were an all-time career high for him. That also shows how much Pierce had grown into an all-around player that was willing to involve his teammates in the offense despite how much as he wanted to score the ball himself. However, the Celtics finished with a record of 36-46. They barely made the postseason as the eighth seed.

The Celtics' fortunes did not change in the playoffs as they struggled more than they ever did that season. The top-seeded Indiana Pacers easily defeated them in four games. They did not even put up much of a fight as the Pacers beat them by double digits in all four games. Paul Pierce tried his best, but he was a one-man team trying to dig out his crew from a deep grave. He averaged 20.8 points and 8.8 rebounds while shooting 34.2% from the field in that sweep.

Enter Doc Rivers

After a disastrous and ineffective year during the 2003-04 season, the Boston Celtics' fortunes would take a turn for the better when they hired former NBA player Doc Rivers as the new head coach of the Green Team. Aside from that, they also acquired capable of youngsters named Al Jefferson, Tony Allen, and Delonte West to complement Paul Pierce, as well as Raef LaFrentz, veteran former superstar point guard Gary Payton, and sixth man Ricky Davis. It was also the first time in a very long while that Paul Pierce had a solid group of capable role players that could help him get Boston to new heights.

In that first season under Rivers, Paul Pierce played the role of the all-around star very well since he did not have to shoulder the full burden of the offensive load. Nevertheless, he would still take over games when he was needed. In his first game that season, he scored 35 points while grabbing 13 rebounds and dishing out eight dimes versus the 76ers in a loss. He would get his first win of the season in the third game as he recorded 28 points, ten rebounds, and eight assists in a 34-point win against the New York Knicks.

In a tight loss to the Washington Wizards on November 17, 2004, Paul Pierce had 37 points and eight rebounds in 43 minutes of action. As the team adjusted to the new system, the Boston Celtics were just trading wins with losses at that early point of the season. Pierce would find himself with mediocre scoring numbers despite contributing to the other aspects of the game such as rebounding and passing.

On December 13, Pierce would have a very efficient shooting night by making 12 of his 17 attempts from the field to score 33 points in a win over the LA Clippers. In a battle versus LeBron James and the Cavaliers on December 18, Pierce had 34 points, seven rebounds, and six assists in a win. On January 3, 2005, he had his first triple-double of the season when he recorded 19 points, ten rebounds, and ten assists in an 18-point win versus the New Orleans Hornets.

On February 2, 2005, he had 28 points, ten rebounds, ten assists, and four steals in a blowout 21-point win over the New Jersey Nets. That was his second triple-double of the season. A few days later, he put up 32 points on 8 out of 16 shooting from the floor and 15 out of 16 from the free throw line to win against the Minnesota Timberwolves by merely 3 points. Three days after that, he almost had another triple-double when he recorded 25 points, ten rebounds, and nine dimes in a win over the LA Clippers. Pierce was then selected to his fourth consecutive All-Star Game appearance as he was quickly becoming one of the favorite stars of the league. Under Rivers, Pierce was not only a great scorer, he was a terrific all-around player that could make plays for his teammates while defending at a high level.

Late in February, Pierce had 29 points, nine rebounds, and seven assists as the Celtics won a rivalry game versus Kobe

Bryant and the Los Angeles Lakers. The Truth would then lead his team to a seven-game winning streak in March. In one of those wins, Pierce had 38 points and 12 rebounds against the defending champions in a two-point win on March 11. After that, Pierce and the Celtics won more games than they lost and were poised to become one of the top-seeded teams in the East. That was all thanks to the leadership and all-around efforts of Paul Pierce, who flourished under Doc Rivers' mentorship.

Paul Pierce would average 21.6 points, 6.6 rebounds, and 4.2 assists at the end of the regular season. Though his scoring numbers seemed lower than his previous four seasons, his field goal percentage was up to 45.5% after a dismal clip the last season. Also, Pierce was playing only an average of 36 minutes per game, which was his lowest since his second season in the NBA. The Truth was also beginning to trust his teammates under the new system employed by Rivers. Because of that, the Boston Celtics ended the regular season with a record of 45-37, which earned them the third seed in the Eastern Conference.

Paul Pierce and his Boston Celtics would have a chance to redeem their loss via a sweep by the Pacers in the 2004 playoffs when they were matched with Indiana again in the first round of the 2005 playoffs. They were the higher-seeded team, which meant that they were in the better position to proceed to the next round. Pierce would love to come back to the Eastern Conference Finals for the first time since 2002.

In Game 1 of that series, Boston drew first blood as they defeated the Pacers by 20 points. Paul Pierce only had to score 12 points in that match, but he did have nine rebounds, five assists, and five steals in that win. Pierce would personally bounce back in Game 2 when he scored 33 points on 9 out of 16 shooting from the field. However, the Pacers took that game by three points as the Celtics lost home court advantage in the series.

Indiana would get a blowout win on their own home floor as they defeated the Celtics by 23 in Game 3. Pierce was limited to 19 points in that game as he could not even get looks for his shots. Pierce and company would retake home court advantage as they tied the series up with a win in Game 4. The Truth had 30 points, seven rebounds, and eight assists in that 31-point blowout win. He would then score 27 in Game 5 as they were seeking to retake the series lead. However, the Pacers took that game by seven points.

In Game 6, Paul Pierce would not allow the Indiana Pacers to beat them again. He tried his best to stretch the series to at least one more win. Paul Pierce had a good all-around game in that quest to force Game 7 as he had 20 points, 11 rebounds, six assists, and four steals in 44 minutes of action. The Celtics managed to push the series to a do-or-die series-clincher. In Game 7, however, the Boston Celtics seemed as if they ran out of gas. Pierce himself would only score 19 points as he attempted merely 13 shots from the floor. In the end, the Indiana Pacers took that game and the series with a 27-point win. Though Paul Pierce tried his best to contribute in every facet of the game that season, it still was not enough to get over the hump.

Missing the Playoffs

After the loss to the Pacers in the 2005 playoffs, the Boston Celtics made several roster changes that made the team look like an entirely different one compared to the group of guys that had made it all the way to the Eastern Conference Finals in 2002. Doc Rivers was working with young guys like Delonte West, Ryan Gomes, Kendrick Perkins, Tony Allen, and Al Jefferson. Paul Pierce and Ricky Davis were the only capable scorers among the few veteran players on the roster. However, Davis missed a lot of games that season because of injuries. As such, Pierce was left to carry the team on his back again.

Paul Pierce opened the 2005-06 season by scoring 30 points and grabbing 12 rebounds in a blowout win versus the New York Knicks. He would then have 28 points in a loss to the Detroit Pistons before scoring 32 as the Celtics were defeated by the Charlotte Bobcats. Later in the month of November, Pierce would explode for 43 points in a loss to the Chicago Bulls. He made 12 of his 21 attempts from the field, 5 of his 8 shots from the three-point line, and 14 of his 18 charity shots. He also had 11 rebounds, five assists, and four steals in that game.

On December 21, he would then score 30 points in a big win versus the Utah Jazz. That was merely a prelude for things to come as he would put up 43 points five days later. In that loss to the Seattle Sonics, Paul Pierce made 13 of his 25 field goal attempts while draining 16 of his 21 shots from the foul line. On January 13, 2006, he barely missed a triple-double when he put up 18 points, nine rebounds, and ten assists in a one-point loss to the Philadelphia 76ers. Pierce made only 4 of his 20 shots in that game as he would sometimes struggle on the scoring end.

On February 1, The Truth would explode again as he scored 40 points. In that loss to the Phoenix Suns, Pierce made 14 of his 27 shots from the field and 4 of his 8 attempts from beyond the three-point line. Three days later, he scored 37 points in what would be the first game of six consecutive outings of scoring at least 30 points. In that loss to the Magic, Pierce was 13 of 30 from the floor. Pierce would then score 35 points in a 32-point blowout win over the Portland Trailblazers on February 10 after he scored 31 in a loss to the Miami Heat. He would then score 31 again as the Boston Celtics won a game versus the Orlando Magic. But those were not the best performances of that six-game scoring stretch.

On February 15, Paul Pierce would record a new career high of 50 points in a loss to the Cleveland Cavaliers, taking the matchup against LeBron James personally. As we have seen historically and in later seasons, Pierce always performed well versus LeBron as they were arguably the two best small forwards of that era. The Truth made 17 of his 36 field goal attempts while hitting 16 of his 20 free throws. He also had 7 rebounds and 8 assists in that double-overtime game. James had a triple-double which included 43 points, 12 rebounds, and 11 assists in that match. Though Pierce lost that battle, he further solidified his claim as one of the best small forwards of that era as he was named to the All-Star team for the fifth consecutive season.

On February 24, Pierce would go for 37 points, 7 rebounds, and 7 assists in a win over the Portland Trailblazers. That was the start of eight games of Pierce scoring at least 30 points. He would then have 39 on 12 of 20 shooting from the field in a win over the rival Los Angeles Lakers team. Kobe had 40 in that fantastic matchup. Pierce would go for 38 in a loss to the Miami Heat before going for 31 points in a win over the Indiana Pacers on March 3. Paul Pierce would then score 33 and 31 in the next two games before having a triple-double of 31 points, 12 rebounds, and 10 assists in the final game of the seven-game scoring stretch. The Boston Celtics won six of those eight outings. Those eight straight games of scoring at least 30 points were a Boston Celtics franchise record. Among the many great players that Boston had seen wearing their green uniform, it was Paul Pierce who set that record.

Paul Pierce averaged a career high in points with 26.8 in that season. He also had 6.7 rebounds, 4.7 assists, and 1.4 steals while shooting 47.1% from the field and 35.4% from the three-point line. Despite the career numbers that Pierce had that season, he was back to being a one-man team as the younger members of the Boston Celtics were too raw and inexperienced to back their superstar up. The Celtics would miss the playoffs with a record of 33 wins against 49 losses.

Missing the Playoffs Again, Injury Season, the Dark Before the Dawn

The 2006-07 season would prove to be the toughest in Paul Pierce's career as an NBA player. It would also become the toughest one for the Celtics since they acquired Pierce back in 1998. The tough season started when Red Auerbach, the man that had brought countless championships to the Boston Celtics as a coach and executive, died at the age of 89. Red had always been an inspirational figure for the Celtics' championship traditions. But his death would not be the only tough part of that season. They were in for one of the worst seasons in franchise history.

Despite the impending doom that the Boston Celtics were about to face in that season, Paul Pierce continued to be his usual stellar self. In his first game of the season, Pierce would go for 28 points and a career-high 19 rebounds versus the New Orleans Hornets in a tough loss. The Celtics would open the season with three straight losses despite Pierce putting up high numbers. He even had 23 points, 12 rebounds, and five assists in their third game. After that, The Truth would go for 35 points, 13 rebounds, and six assists as he led the Celtics to their first win of the season against the Charlotte Bobcats. On November 15, 2006,

Paul Pierce would put up 32 points as he made 11 of his 19 field goal attempts and 8 of his 9 free throw shots in a 26-point win against the Indiana Pacers.

Paul Pierce would put up 34 points, seven rebounds, and seven assists as he led his Boston Celtics to a win over the Milwaukee Bucks on November 25. On December 8, he would go for 36 points on 10 of 14 shooting from the field and 7 out of 14 shooting from beyond the arc in a loss to the Phoenix Suns. After that, he led Boston to a five-game winning streak. He had three amazing highlight games in that streak. He first delivered 31 points versus the New York Knicks. After that, he had 38 points, 8 rebounds, and 9 assists against the Denver Nuggets before putting up 35 points and 11 rebounds on the Charlotte Bobcats on December 16. However, Paul Pierce's luck would take a turn for the worse after that. He would miss almost two months of action because of an injury caused by a stress reaction in his foot.

Paul Pierce would come back to action on February 9, 2007. He would only play 20 minutes that game while scoring merely 9 points for the reeling Boston Celtics team that could not win games without their superstar. Pierce quickly got back to superstar form as he delivered 29 points on 9 out of 16 in his second game back from injury. After that match, he had 32 points on Valentines Day against the Bucks in a 20-point win. Despite another stellar statistical season for Paul Pierce, he missed the All-Star Game for the first time since 2002 because of the games he missed. Had he been healthy, he would have surely been an All-Star for the sixth consecutive season.

Pierce would continue to play his best brand of basketball even after the All-Star break. He even led the Celtics to a four-game winning streak, which was a rarity because of how bad their season turned out to be. Despite playing hard every single night, it was clear that his foot was bothering him as he found it difficult to explode for big scoring games. On March 17, Pierce finally broke the 30-point barrier for the first time in almost a month as he scored 30 points on the San Antonio Spurs in a rare win. His final game of the season was on March 28 when he put up 32 points against the Orlando Magic in a nine-point win.

After that game against the Magic, Pierce would miss the remaining games because of his foot injury. He averaged 25 points, 5.9 rebounds, and 4.1 assists while shooting 43.9% from the floor in the 47 games that he played the entire season. The Boston Celtics would end up with a record of 24-58, which was one of the worst records in the league at that time. They even lost 18 consecutive games, which was the highest streak the franchise had ever hadstruggling mightily with a roster of youngsters like rookie Rajon Rondo, Leon Powe, and Sebastian Telfair. As they say, the night is darkest just before the dawn. But the only bright spot for the Celtics in that awful year was the breakout season of promising big man Al Jefferson. One other bright spot was that the Celtics were able to get the fifth pick in the 2008 NBA Draft as they had the chance of landing a promising rookie to play alongside Pierce. It would turn out that nothing would be brighter than what happened to the Boston Celtics during the 2007 offseason.

Forming the New Boston Big Three

In the offseason before the 2007-08 season, Paul Pierce was as disappointed and as frustrated as he had ever been. He was disappointed in himself for being unable to lead the Boston Celtics to relevance again and for not being able to stay healthy in the past season. Had Pierce been healthy, he could have led his team to a playoff appearance. And even if he made the postseason, there was no masking his frustrations with having to lead a group of young guys as the lone superstar. He had absolutely no capable veterans helping him, much less talented All-Stars. He was frustrated with how the Celtics front office could not bring him help. At that point, he was already unsure of his future with the Boston Celtics. He was still in the prime of his career and was ready to start from scratch elsewhere if given the opportunity to do so.[xiv]

The Boston Celtics had a chance to rebuild through the draft because of two young prospects who were poised to become game changers in the NBA. Greg Oden and Kevin Durant were slated to be the first and second picks of that 2007 NBA Draft. Because the Celtics had the second worst record in the league, they had a good chance of adding any of those young prospects. However, they fell to the number five pick. With no transcendent talent predicted to be available at that pick, the Celtics were in the mood to trade their spot at 2007 NBA Draft.[xiv]

The bright spot for the Boston Celtics at that point was that Paul Pierce was not the only disgruntled and frustrated superstar in the NBA. Two other stars were looking to move elsewhere because of their respective teams' lack of success. First, there was Kevin Garnett. KG was arguably the best power forward during his peak. He scored from anywhere on the floor, rebounded at a high rate, defended every other position, and made plays for other people. Because of his leadership, he was the 2004 NBA MVP as he led the Minnesota Timberwolves to the NBA's best record. However, the Wolves would fall apart from then on. Garnett was frustrated with how he could not even make the postseason.

Danny Ainge, the Celtics' general manager, took advantage of that situation. He had been teammates with Kevin McHale, the Timberwolves' executive. As such, they remained good friends throughout the season. Fearing that KG may opt out of his contract after the 2007-08 season, the Timberwolves and Celtics discussed trades that involved their superstar. There were other possible destinations like the Los Angeles Lakers and the Cleveland Cavaliers. But the Celtics were the frontrunners. However, trade talks were difficult since the Minnesota Timberwolves wanted as much as they could take for one of the NBA's best players.[xiv]

The second player that wanted to move elsewhere was Ray Allen. At that point in the NBA, Allen was the best shooter in the league. He consistently made more three-pointers than any other player year in and year out. He was also a prolific scorer aside from making the All-Star team every season. Allen had seen a good amount of postseason success when he was with the Milwaukee Bucks. He later moved on to join the Seattle SuperSonics. However, the Sonics were not the ideal fit for him as they struggled to make playoff appearances. Since Seattle had the second pick in the 2007 NBA Draft, they were looking to rebuild with their draft choice. Because of that, they agreed to send Ray Allen in exchange for the Celtics' number five draft pick, Wally Szczerbiak, and Delonte West.[xiv]

Paul Pierce was excited with the acquisition of Ray Allen. With Allen in the fold, he could focus on playing the small forward spot instead of occasionally sliding into the shooting guard role from time-to-time. Allen could also stretch the floor to allow Pierce to have a lot of space to make moves for scoring opportunities. Finally, he had another All-Star that could alleviate him of a lot of offensive burdens and defensive pressure. But the Boston Celtics were not done yet.

Trade talks with the Minnesota Timberwolves revived as the Wolves' team owner Glen Taylor wanted to start fresh with younger talent. Though Garnett was initially uncomfortable about the idea of leaving Minnesota, he was interested in playing for the Celtics because of how much All-Star talent Boston had after acquiring Ray Allen. After several weeks of deliberation, the cards were in play. The Minnesota Timberwolves would be receiving developing big man Al Jefferson together with Theo Ratliff, Gerald Green, and two other role players. The Wolves also received the players that the Celtics drafted in the recent NBA Draft. In exchange for that, the Boston Celtics received Kevin Garnett, one of the most dominating superstars of that era.[xiv]

With the acquisition of Ray Allen and Kevin Garnett, the Boston Celtics were ready to roll into the new season with the Big Three of the new era. However, not a lot of people initially thought that those three players would gel immediately and dominate the NBA. The three superstars never had the opportunity to play with players of such talent. Garnett was used to doing everything on the floor for the Celtics. Allen was used to being the go-to guy in any situation. Meanwhile, Pierce was always the leader and the primary weapon of the Boston Celtics.

What was unaccounted for was that how hungry for a championship those three players were. They were in the prime of their respective careers and were already mature enough to put all ego aside for a chance to win a title. The chemistry grew even better when the Boston Celtics flew to Europe for a few exhibition games and training sessions. It was at that time when the roles were set. Kevin Garnett would handle the defensive duties and emotional leadership on the floor. Ray Allen was the designated shooter and the guy they would give the ball to whenever they needed a game-winner. Paul Pierce was the overall leader, the go-to guy on offense, and the man that would bail them out whenever they needed points on the board. The table was set for the Boston Celtics as the day had completely dawned on them after the darkest hours were all but gone. The rest of the NBA teams were on notice.

Winning the 2008 NBA Title

Since Paul Pierce was playing with two of the best players of that era of the NBA, he had no reason to carry the team by himself. He had no reason to do everything else on the floor as much as he did in previous seasons. Because of that, Pierce had only one thing to do – score big shots. The Truth did just that as helped the Boston Celtics to get a hot start in the season with nine straight wins to no loss.

In the first game of that 9-0 opening record, Paul Pierce had 28 points, five rebounds, and four assists against the Washington Wizards. He would score 26 points on 10 out of 15 shooting in their third win, which was against the Denver Nuggets. On November 10, 2007, Pierce would score 28 points on the New Jersey Nets before putting up 31 points, 11 rebounds, and six assists in a 15-point win over the Indiana Pacers three days later. Pierce would only combine for 27 points on 11 out of 22 shooting in the next two games to round up the nine-game winning start. He would score 28 points when the Orlando Magic broke their great season start on November 18.

In their next 11 games, the Boston Celtics would only lose one game as they started the season going 18-2 through their first 20 outings. Pierce had seven splendid performances along the way. He had his second double-double game on November 21 when he had 19 points and ten rebounds. Pierce would then contribute 21 points to the 45-point embarrassing win over the New York Knicks. On December 5, he had 19 points and 12 assists to lead the way for the Boston Celtics versus the Philadelphia 76ers. In his 20th game of the season, Paul Pierce had 26 points as the Celtics won their 18th game.

On December 14, Paul Pierce scored 32 points as he hit five three-pointers in a 22-point win versus the Milwaukee Bucks. On December 27, Pierce hit his then-season high of 37 points as he led Boston in a win over the Sonics. Two games later, Pierce rounded up the year by scoring 33 points against the Los Angeles Lakers in a rivalry game. He would have 19 points, nine rebounds, and seven assists to lead the Boston Celtics to their 29th win on January 5, 2008. The Celtics were 29-3 to start their first 32 games with Pierce playing.

Paul Pierce would be on cruise control from the onset of the New Year as he learned to trust his teammates more. Not only were the Big Three playing at a high level, but the rest of the Celtics were also full of confidence especially with the number of wins they were piling up. Role players such as Rajon Rondo, James Posey, Eddie House, and Tony Allen were all contributing to the cause of the Boston Celtics as they learned not to lean on their Big Three so much. But Paul Pierce would still have his usual explosions from time-to-time.

On February 10, Paul Pierce put up 35 points on 11 out of 18 shooting from the floor and 5 out of 9 from the three-point line to lead the way in a win over the San Antonio Spurs. He would then have 28 points and 12 rebounds in their next game, which was a win over the Indiana Pacers. With those performances, Paul Pierce solidified his name as one of the three Celtic players named to the Eastern Conference All-Star squad. While he had the experience of playing with another All-Star when Antoine Walker was in his prime years, it was the first time that Pierce had the opportunity to play with two other star players at the peak of their careers.

Things turned sour for a while after the All-Star break as the Boston Celtics lost their first three games to start the second half of the season. They would break the three-game losing streak by defeating the Portland Trailblazers by 10 points on February 24. Paul Pierce led the way with 30 points, seven rebounds, and five assists as he made 12 of his 14 field goal attempts. He would lead the team to a 10-game winning streak. In one of those wins, he had 30 points on 10 out of 19 shooting from the field versus the Atlanta Hawks. He would have a double-double performance of 14 points and 11 assists as they beat the Sonics by 29 big points on March 12.

Paul Pierce would be a steady force for the Boston Celtics and was one of the main catalysts for a great start and a good end to the season. The Celtics were no doubt the best team in the NBA that season as they finished with a record of 66 wins to 16 losses. That was the biggest single-season turnaround in NBA history. But that would not mean anything without an NBA title. Paul Pierce led the team in scoring by averaging 19.6 points together with 5.1 rebounds and 4.5 assists. He was nominated to the All-NBA Third Team. His statistics may have looked lower than the numbers he put up in previous seasons. However, it was not because he slacked off. It was because he was playing alongside two other great players, namely Ray Allen and Kevin Garnett, who won the Defensive Player of the Year award that season. The offensive load was spread across the Big Three, but

Pierce's scoring numbers still shone brighter than any other Celtic.

Though the Celtics were the best team in basketball in the regular season, the postseason was not as easy as they would think. In the first round, the Atlanta Hawks pushed them to the limit. It took seven games for the Celtics to dispatch them Boston won Games 1 and 2 easily. Pierce even only had to combine for 30 points in those easy wins. However, Atlanta defended their home court well to tie the series up at two wins apiece after Game 4. Pierce went for a combined performance of 35 points in those two losses in Atlanta.

The Truth would not let the Hawks take the series lead. He had 22 points, seven rebounds, and six assists after a blowout win in Game 5. As the Celtics were looking to beat the Hawks in Game 6, Atlanta would show how well they defend their home floor by winning the game by three. Pierce was limited to 17 points in that match. Despite a valiant fight, the Hawks would fall from the sky in Game 7 when the Celtics stomped over them with their star experience and championship hunger. Boston won Game 7 by 34. Paul Pierce had 22 points in that game.

The second round would not be so easy either; the Celtics went on to face LeBron James and the Cleveland Cavaliers. LeBron was beginning to become the best player on the planet during that season, but he was a one-man team confronted with a core of three superstars itching to win their first title. Everything was clicking in Game 1 of that series as the Boston Celtics won by 4 points despite a tough shooting night for Pierce, who only had 4 points. The Celtics would defend their home floor once again as they routed the Cavs by 19 points in Game 2. Paul Pierce had 19 points on 7 out of 13 shooting from the field in that game.

LeBron James was not known as one of the greatest players in the NBA for nothing. He and his team dominated the Celtics back in Cleveland as they also defended their home court. Pierce did not do well in either of those games, either. He combined for merely 27 points in those two losses as the Cavaliers tied the series 2-2. Paul Pierce bounced back from his pedestrian performances throughout the playoffs. He ended a Game 5 win by putting 29 points up on the board. The Celtics were up 3-2 after that.

Much like how the Hawks did it, the Cleveland Cavaliers protected all of their home games in that series. They defeated the Celtics by 5 points in Game 6 to force a do-or-die Game 7. It was during Game 7 that Paul Pierce showed why he was one of the biggest shot makers and big game players in the NBA. He went toe-to-toe with LeBron James as he tried to match the Cavs' superstar point for point. Whenever James would make a shot, Pierce would make one even bigger. In the end, LeBron finished with 45 points. Meanwhile, Pierce hit 12 of his 23 field goal attempts and 4 of his 6 three-pointers to score 41 points. Though LeBron won the individual matchup, Pierce's team won the game and the series.

Paul Pierce was back in the Eastern Conference Finals for the first time since 2002. In the way of his quest to making the NBA Finals for the first time were the Detroit Pistons, who were a perennial Eastern powerhouse. In Game 1 of that series, Pierce scored 22 to help his team win the game by nine. He then went on to score 26 in Game 2, but it was in vain as Detroit tied the series with a win. The Celtics would finally win a game away from home as they took Game 3 away from the tough Detroit Pistons. Pierce would score only 11 points in that match.

The Pistons would take Game 4 with a 19-point win. They defended Boston well that game as they limited Pierce to shooting 3 of his 14 bricks for merely 16 points. However, the Celtics would show their grit and their hunger in Games 5 and 6. The Celtics would win Game 5 by 4 points as their superstars were running on all cylinders. For the sixth game of the series in

Detroit, Paul Pierce would score 27 points and grab eight rebounds to help the Boston Celtics to win the series in six games. They finally made it all the way to the NBA Finals for the first time since Larry Bird, Kevin McHale, and Robert Parish were dominating the league as a trio.

In the NBA Finals, age-old rivalries were renewed as the Boston Celtics clashed with the Los Angeles Lakers for league supremacy. Those two teams were the winningest teams regarding championships in the history of the NBA. Led by the 2008 MVP Kobe Bryant, the Celtics had their hands full guarding one of the best scorers and greatest players the league has ever seen. As the Lakers only had one superstar to push the team to a title, the Celtics had three stars all hungry for that first ring.

Paul Pierce would show how hungry he was for a title as he scored 22 points on 7 out of 10 shooting from the field in Game 1. He would only play 31 minutes as the Celtics opted to play defensive-minded wingmen to cover Bryant. He was also injured in the third quarter but came back later to score 15 of his 22 points in the third canto. The defensive strategy and Pierce's clutch performance all worked as Boston drew first blood. Pierce would then go into Game 2 to score 28 points on 9 out of

16 shooting from the floor. He also dished out eight assists to help his team win the game for a 2-0 lead in the series.

In Game 3 in Los Angeles, Paul Pierce was limited to one of his worst games in the playoffs. He would score merely 6 points on 2 out of 14 shooting as the Lakers had defensive looks of their own for The Truth. Los Angeles would win that game by six points. Pierce would then lead a comeback in Game 4 with 20 points. That win put the Celtics up 3-1 in the series

The Lakers would inch within a game closer to the Boston Celtics by winning Game 5 by five points. The Celtics tried to come back from a huge deficit that game to win. However, they fell short. Pierce had 38 big points in that game as he made 10 of his 22 shots from the field. The Boston Celtics return home for Game 6 as they had all the chances in the world to secure the NBA title. Pierce, though limited to 17 points that game, dished out ten assists to the clicking Boston Celtics, who were draining three-pointers like cash money throughout the match. The Lakers did not know what hit them as they lost Game 6 by an embarrassing 39 points.

With that win, the Boston Celtics secured their 18th championship banner, the most in NBA history. Though it was an all-around effort for every Celtic, it was Paul Pierce who was named the NBA Finals MVP for his stellar approach in leading his team and for the many big shots he had made throughout the series. Pierce, Garnett, and Allen won their first championship rings as they ended a 22-year title drought for the Boston Celtics.

This was the same Paul Pierce that could not make the varsity team in high school. This was the same guy that almost gut cut from the basketball team when he was a teenager. Now, Pierce could relish at the fact that all the hard work and setbacks he faced led to the moment he raised his NBA championship trophy and his Finals MVP award. There were no doubts about him at that moment because he had reached the pinnacle of basketball success. With all the confidence in the world, Pierce would later exclaim on that night that he was the best player in the world. Though that was debatable on a general basis, on that night, nobody could bring down the confidence of The Truth as he had just become an NBA champion.

Failed Attempt to Defend the NBA Championship

The Boston Celtics decided to keep the core that had helped them win the NBA title. They were still the most complete team as far as veteran leadership, championship experience, and overall talent. The Boston Celtics were headed for a season with a stronger resolve and with the same kind of hunger that had brought them an NBA title. Paul Pierce, Kevin Garnett, and Ray Allen were still hungry for more. The defending champions would not yield to any competitor.

Paul Pierce, at the age of 31, was slowly moving past his prime years as a basketball competitor. But he could still score and perform with the great ones that season as he prepared to defend his NBA title. In his first game of the 2008-09 season, he scored 27 points in a win over the Cleveland Cavaliers. Several games later, he had 36 points versus the Toronto Raptors. After that game, he scored 34 over the Atlanta Hawks. Both great scoring games came with wins. Given Pierce's age and with the All-Star cast he was playing alongside with, it is still amazing to see him put up high-scoring outputs from time to time.

Pierce would then have 28 points, seven rebounds, and six assists as he led his team to a win over the Milwaukee Bucks on November 5. He was ultra-efficient as he made 5 of his 9 field goal attempts, 4 of his 4 of his three-pointers, and 14 of his 15 free throw shots. While Pierce was doing all that and a lot more, the Boston Celtics were still winning at a rate similar to their championship season. They won 18 of their first 20 games to start the season. But the winning did not stop there.

The Boston Celtics would win their next nine games as they started out with a record of 27-2. That was the best season start in NBA history. In the middle of all that, Paul Pierce was at his best. Though his scoring numbers were a bit underwhelming for a man of his caliber, he did everything else right as he dished out five or more assists in six of those nine wins. His best scoring game in that stretch was when he put up 28 points against the New Orleans Hornets on December 12.

After the hot start to the season, Paul Pierce and the Boston Celtics would slow down a bit as the New Year dawned. Though they would win their first game of 2009, they dropped the next four though Pierce was scoring well. He had 31 points and seven rebounds in a loss to the New York Knicks before putting up 28 and 26 in the next two games, which were losses to the Charlotte Bobcats and the Houston Rockets. After the Celtics had broken their losing streak on January 11, Paul Pierce came to score big in the following game. The Truth exploded for 39 points as he made 13 of his 26 field goals and 10 of his 11 free throws versus the Toronto Raptors in a six-point win. On February 1, Pierce scored 36 points on the Minnesota Timberwolves as he hit 13 of his 24 attempts from the field and 9 of his 9 shots from the charity stripe. He would score 29 in the following game in a one-point win over the Philadelphia 76ers.

On February 11, Pierce would score 30 on the Hornets before putting up 31 on the Dallas Mavericks the following day. Both were wins as Paul Pierce secured his seventh All-Star Game appearance.

However, things quickly turned for the worse after the All-Star break. The Boston Celtics would lose Kevin Garnett in their first game since coming back from the midseason break. KG would miss the rest of the regular season as he recovered from injury. It was up to Paul Pierce, Ray Allen, and rising point guard Rajon Rondo to pick up the pieces for the Boston Celtics after their Big Ticket went down.

Without Garnett, the Boston Celtics started to lose more games than they had earlier in the season. Despite that, they were still an elite team in the NBA and one of the top playoff contenders in the East. Best of all, they were still the NBA champions until someone could dethrone them. Pierce was in the middle of all of it as he had to score more without KG in the fold. In a win over the New Jersey Nets on March 4, he had 31 points on 12 out of 14 shooting from the field. He would then score 29 against the Cleveland Cavaliers in their next game as Pierce always played well against LeBron.

Later on March 17, Paul Pierce had what would be his best two-game stretch in that season. He had 37 points and seven rebounds in that loss to the Chicago Bulls as he made 13 of his 24 field goals and 8 of 8 free throw attempts. In the next game, Pierce made 14 of 23 attempts from the field as he ended a win over the Miami Heat with 36 points, 11 rebounds, and 5 assists. Kevin Garnett briefly came back at that period but was immediately shut down for the entire season as he was required to rest even more to recover from his injury.

Nevertheless, Paul Pierce still did his best to lead the Celtics for the remainder of the season without the emotional defensive leader on the floor. He would lead the team to a record of 7-1 in their final eight games of the season. In six of those games, he scored at least 20 points. At the end of the 2008-09 regular season, Paul Pierce averaged 20.5 points, 5.6 rebounds, and 3.6 assists while shooting 45.7% from the floor and 39.1% from the three-point line to lead the Boston Celtics to a record of 62-20. He made the All-NBA Second Team. As the second seed in the Eastern Conference playoff picture, the Celtics had an excellent chance to defend their NBA title especially with how they had home court advantage until the Eastern Conference Finals.

The first-round series of the playoffs against the young and hungry Chicago Bulls was one of the best playoff series in NBA history. The Bulls managed to pull off an upset win over the Celtics in Game 1 as they forced overtime to win the game by two points. Rookie of the Year Derrick Rose had 36 points and 11 rebounds while Pierce had 23 points on 21 shot attempts. Game 2 was just as close as the first game as both teams played each other blow-for-blow. With Paul Pierce struggling for 18 points, the Celtics leaned on Ray Allen to battle with Ben Gordon in a shootout. Allen ended with 30 points while Gordon finished with 42. However, the Celtics escaped with a three-point win.

The Boston Celtics would not allow the Bulls to play them close in Game 3 of that series. Paul Pierce led his team to a victory with a 24-point output. The Celtics defeated their counterparts by 21 points in that outing. The Bulls would fight back in Game 4 as they pushed the Celtics to two overtimes. Pierce finished with 29 points though he and his team lost that battle by three points. Game 5 was another overtime classic where Boston defeated Chicago by two points in the extra period. Pierce finished with 26 points in that match.

Because two overtimes were not enough, Game 6 had to go to triple-overtime. Ray Allen, who hit nine three-pointers in that game, was the star of the show. Meanwhile, Paul Pierce had 22 points as he deferred to his hot-shooting teammate. Despite that historic match, the Bulls forced Game 7 with a one-point win in that matchup. The Celtics refused to exit the playoffs early and pushed the Bulls to a hard-fought Game 7. Though Chicago fought valiantly, Boston came out with a 10-point victory. Paul Pierce had 20 points in that closeout win.

In the second round, the Boston Celtics faced off against the dominant Dwight Howard and the Orlando Magic. However, without their best interior defender Kevin Garnett, the Celtics struggled to contain the scoring and rebounding prowess that Howard had inside the paint. They would lose Game 1 by five points before winning Game 2 by 18. Pierce only had three points in that win. The Celtics would only win two of the next five games as Dwight Howard proved to be too much for the Boston Celtics' interior defenders. It could also be that the aging Celtics had already run out of gas after a historic series against the Chicago Bulls in the first round. With that series loss to the Magic, the Boston Celtics were dethroned as NBA champions. Things would have been a lot different had Kevin Garnett been healthy. They had a chance to repeat as champions.

Return to the NBA Finals

Kevin Garnett was back to full health coming into the 2009-10 season, rejoining the Big Three together with Ray Allen and

Paul Pierce. However, the Big Three was slowly becoming a foursome with the steady rise of Rajon Rondo. With the Boston Celtics fully healthy and reinforced, they had as good of a chance as anybody to get a shot at another NBA title.

Paul Pierce, though, was still the most important piece of the Celtic puzzle as he continued to score in bunches for his team. He had 23 points and 11 rebounds in his first game of the season. He would be instrumental in leading the Celtics to a 6-0 start to the season. On November 22, 2009, Pierce would score 33 points together with nine rebounds and six assists as the Celtics won a close game against the New York Knicks. He scored 27 points in the following game. The Celtics, at that point, seemed unbeatable again as they started the season winning 23 of their first 28 games.

From that point on, Doc Rivers made a decision that would adversely affect the regular season performance of the team, but would benefit the Celtics in the long run. The Celtic core was an aging one. Paul Pierce was 32, KG was turning 34 while Ray Allen was 34. Though they were still dangerous at an individual level, they were at the point in their careers where their minutes should be monitored closely for preservation for the playoffs. Doc Rivers would decrease his starters' minutes.

Despite the decline in minutes, Pierce was still performing well for a man past his prime years. On January 29, 2010, he put up a season-high 35 points on 11 of 15 shooting from the field and 12 of 13 made attempts from the charity stripe in a loss to the Atlanta Hawks. After that, he would fall to mediocre performances as the Celtics were technically trading wins with losses. Nevertheless, Pierce was named as an All-Star that season for the eighth time in his career. Paul Pierce even participated in the Three-Point Shootout during the All-Star Weekend as he previously proclaimed that he was the best shooter on the planet. That was a big statement coming from him considering he had to duel with teammate Ray Allen in that contest. That goes to show how confident of a player Paul Pierce is. For that night at least, he was right in proclaiming himself as the best shooter in the league when he took home the trophy. That was the kind of man Paul Pierce is. He would utter big statements, but would back them up with even greater performances.

Paul Pierce averaged 18.3 points, 4.4 rebounds, and 3.1 assists while shooting a career-best 47.2% from the floor in that season. The Boston Celtics would go on to win 50 of their 82 games even after a hot start to the season. The reason was that starters were preserved for the playoffs as the bench saw more minutes during the regular season. Nevertheless, the Celtics were still a top contender in the East as they secured the fourth seed.

It turned out that the rest was all the doctor (Doc) ordered as the Celtics seemed fresh and rejuvenated in the postseason. They quickly dispatched Dwyane Wade and the Miami Heat in the first round, only losing one game in that series. Pierce performed admirably in Game 3 when the Celtics took an insurmountable 3-0 lead over the Miami Heat. Paul Pierce had 32 points on 11 of 23 shooting from the floor and 4 out of 10 from the three-point line to lead his team to a two-point win. He then had 21 points as Boston closed Miami out in Game 5.

The second round was tougher as the Boston Celtics met the top-seeded NBA team with MVP LeBron James leading them. The Cleveland Cavaliers managed to win Game 1 on their home floor by 8 points as The Truth was kept from scoring well with merely 13 points in that game. Pierce would again be limited to a poor scoring night in Game 2, but the Celtics played good defense and delivered a balanced offense to beat the Cavs by 18 on their home floor. Cleveland would get revenge by winning Game 3 by 29. At that point, it seemed like the Celtics were too old and too slow to run with the fresher Cavaliers.

However, the Boston Celtics quickly went back to championship form as they defeated the Cavaliers in the next three games to proceed to the Eastern Conference Finals. In Game 4, Paul Pierce finally broke out of his slump as he delivered 21 points, 11 rebounds, and seven assists to lead his team to a 32-point win. He would then contribute to the Celtics' mission of frustrating LeBron James as the MVP quit on his team because of how tightly the Boston defense played.

The Boston Celtics would have a chance to redeem their second round loss in the previous year's postseason as they faced the Orlando Magic in the Eastern Conference Finals. This time they proved that Orlando was only able to beat them because Kevin Garnett was not around to patrol the paint the first time. Pierce immediately stamped his class on the Magic by scoring 22 points in the opening game, which was a win for the Green Team. He then had 28 in Game 2 to lead Boston to a 2-0 series lead. In Game 3, he contributed 15 points and nine rebounds as the Celtics went up ahead to an insurmountable 3-0 series lead.

Orlando would not go quietly into the night. Despite 32 points and 11 rebounds from Pierce in Game 4, the Magic managed to stay alive. In Game 5, they would push the series even longer as they defeated Boston by 21 points. But history was not on the side of the Orlando Magic as they would fail to become the only team to have ever come back and win from a 0-3 deficit in a seven-game series. Meanwhile, Paul Pierce was on the side of the Celtics as he proved why he was always known as a big time player. He poured in 31 points and 13 rebounds to lead his team over the Orlando Magic in Game 6. With that win, the Celtics were back in the NBA Finals for the first time since winning it two seasons ago.

The Celtics would meet the Los Angeles Lakers in the 2010 NBA Finals in a virtual rematch of their 2008 meeting. At that point, the Lakers were the defending champions and the higher-seeded team. They had two behemoth 7-foot All-Stars patrolling the paint as Kobe Bryant handled the perimeter. They also had Ron Artest to shadow Paul Pierce at the small forward position. Though it had only been two years since they embarrassed the Lakers in Game 6, the Boston Celtics were now the underdogs against the powerhouse Lakers team.

The Lakers would prove why they were the defending champs when they took Game 1 by 13 points. Pierce would score 24 in that loss. Though The Truth was silent in Game 2 with only 10 points, Ray Allen was clicking from the three-point line as he drained an NBA Finals record of seven three-pointers in a half to lead the way for the Celtics in that win. In Boston, both

Pierce and Allen were silent as the Lakers defended them well enough to gain back home court advantage.

Despite a godly performance from Kobe Bryant in Game 4, Paul Pierce and company played a balanced brand of offense and a suffocating style of defense to take that win away as they tied the series at two wins apiece. Bryant would explode against the Celtics yet again in Game 5. However, he was the only Laker truly clicking from the floor as the Boston Celtics kept everyone else from scoring. The result was a win for both the Celtics team and Paul Pierce, who had 27 points in that game.

As the Celtics rolled into Los Angeles for Games 6 and possibly 7, Lakers head coach Phil Jackson was confident despite the Celtics leading 3-2 in the series. He insisted that the Celtic lead was merely the result of the home court situation. The Celtics were intent on refuting that as they were only a game away from the 19th franchise NBA championship. However, the Lakers found an extra pair of legs as they ran through Boston in Game 6 with a 22-point win. Game 7 was set as the Celtics and the Lakers battled it out in a classic series. The final game was a tight defensive contest where neither side could score on each other. Despite a double-digit lead in the second half for Boston, Los Angeles came back as they banked on the clutch plays of Kobe Bryant and Ron Artest. In the end, a couple of late three-pointers from Artest sealed the deal for the Boston Celtics, who failed to secure their second championship in three seasons. That would be the final time that the new Big Three would come close to winning another title.

Seasons of Falling Short

For the 2010-11 season, the Boston Celtics secured the services of former dominant superstar big man Shaquille O'Neal as Kendrick Perkins was recovering from a serious injury he suffered against the Lakers in their meeting in the 2010 NBA Finals. However, Paul Pierce initially opted out of his contract that season, but subsequently signed with Boston on a four-year contract. With a bolstered lineup that was centered on the foursome of Pierce, Allen, Garnett, and Rondo, the Celtics were still one of the most feared teams in the NBA, even after the Miami Heat were able to form their own Big Three composed of LeBron James, Dwyane Wade, and Chris Bosh.

Pierce and company were not deterred as they opened the season by beating the newly formed super team of the Miami Heat by eight points in their first game of the season. Paul Pierce had 19 points and nine rebounds in that match. Two games later, he would have 25 points, 14 rebounds, and five assists as they defeated the New York Knicks by four points. He would then have 21 and 28 in the next two games, which were both wins. When he scored 28 on the Milwaukee Bucks on November 3, Pierce became one of the few players to score more than 20,000 career points.

Pierce and the Celtics continued their mastery over the Miami Heat by beating them on November 11, 2010. The Truth had 25 points in that game. On November 13, Pierce would then score 28 points as the Celtics defeated the upstart Memphis Grizzlies team by six points before going for 23 in the 31-point win versus the Washington Wizards. On December 1, he had 28 points on 9 out of 11 shooting from the field to win against the Portland Trailblazers. Later that month, Paul Pierce had a good double-double game when he had 32 points and ten rebounds in a win over the New York Knicks. He would go for a triple-double of 18 points, ten rebounds, and 12 assists in a win over Indiana on December 19. On January 2, 2011, Paul Pierce started the New Year right when he scored 30 points on 10 out of 15 shooting in a win over the Toronto Raptors. On January 30, Paul Pierce would then score 32 points in as the Celtics defeated the Los Angeles Lakers by 13 points in a Finals rematch. On February 16, he had 31 points in a win over New Jersey as he secured his ninth overall All-Star appearance.

In his 13th season in the NBA, Paul Pierce averaged 18.9 points, 5.4 rebounds, and 3.3 assists while shooting a new career high of 49.7% from the floor. The Boston Celtics would finish the season with a record of 56-26, which was good enough for the third seed in the Eastern Conference that saw the rise of the Miami Heat and Chicago Bulls as the top contenders.

Paul Pierce and company would easily outplay the much-improved New York Knicks in the first round of the 2011 playoffs. In Game 1, Pierce had 18 points to lead the way for the Celtics to draw first blood. They then raced ahead to 2-0 as The Truth poured in 20 points the next game. In Game 3, everything was clicking for the Boston Celtics and especially for Paul Pierce, who finished with 38 points on 14 out of 19 shooting from the floor and 6 out of 8 from downtown. He would only have 13 points in Game 4 as the Celtics swept the Knicks out of the playoffs.

In the second round, the Celtics were up against the newest Big Three in town as the younger Heat core was looking have the Boston squad cede their dominance over to Miami. With that, Boston never even knew what hit them as the Heat won the two opening games. The Celtics would regroup at home when they won by 16 points. Paul Pierce led the way with 27 points in that win. He would have 27 points again in Game 4, but the Heat took that one. The Miami Heat finally put the aging Celtics to rest after beating them in Game 5 by 10 points. Because of that easy loss to the Heat, the Celtics were quickly criticized because many people believed that the age of their core All-Stars could no longer keep up with the younger superstars of the new generation of NBA players.

After the 2010-11 season, the league went into a lockout which was induced by a labor dispute between the players' union and the NBA team owners. The lockout would finally end in December while the league would start late in that month. The good news for aging teams like the Celtics was that they had plenty of time to rest before the 2011-12 season could get underway. The bad news was that the compressed 66-game schedule meant less rest throughout the rest of the season.

Nevertheless, Paul Pierce remained steadfast and committed to bringing his team back to championship glory. Though he started the season slowly, Pierce would break out of the early slump when he scored 21 points together with eight rebounds in a win over the Washington Wizards. He would then score 24 in the next game. On January 34, Pierce nearly had a triple-double when he had 34 points, eight rebounds, and ten assists in a win over the Washington Wizards. He shot 10 out of 15 from the field and made 12 of his 15 free throw attempts. It was pretty impressive for a 34-year old to get those numbers.

Four days after that, Paul Pierce would have 24 points and ten assists in a win over the Orlando Magic. He then had 28 points, ten rebounds, and eight assists in another near triple-double effort in a win over the Indiana Pacers. The Truth would break the 30-point barrier after scoring 30 points in a win over the Knicks on February 3, 2012. On February 7, Paul Pierce passed Larry Bird for second all-time in the Boston Celtics' franchise career points when he had 15 points, eight rebounds, and nine assists in a win over the Charlotte Bobcats. Considering that Boston had seen its share of great superstars over a long, storied franchise history, it was nothing short of an amazing accomplishment for Paul Pierce. That accomplishment would be compounded when he was chosen to play in his 10th and final All-Star Game.

On March 4, Paul Pierce would score 34 points in a win over New York. He then had 30 in their next game, which was a win over the Houston Rockets. On March 26, he would have a double-double while scoring a new season high. Pierce had 36 points and ten rebounds in a win over the Charlotte Bobcats. That was the middle game of a seven-game streak of scoring at least 20 points for Pierce. On April 17, Pierce would score a new season high when he put up 43 big points in a loss to the Knicks. He made 11 of his 19 attempts from the floor while also making 17 of his 18 shots from the foul line. In the next game, he did not seem tired at all as he put up 29 points and 14 assists in a win over the Orlando Magic.

The Boston Celtics would end the regular season with a record of 39-27, which gave them the fourth seed in the Eastern Conference. Paul Pierce averaged 19.4 points, 5.2 rebounds, and 4.5 assists while shooting 44.3% from the field in what would become his final season as an All-Star. As a player past 34 years of age, Paul Pierce was still putting up incredible numbers for his team as he has been the Celtics' leading scorer since 2001.

Coming into the 2012 playoffs, the Boston Celtics were getting a lot of criticism. Some said they were too old to run with the younger teams in the East. Some said their championship days were well behind them already. They were intent on proving those critics wrong as they squared up against the young Atlanta Hawks in the first round. For a moment, critics were right as the Hawks defeated them in Game 1. The All-Star Paul Pierce only had 12 points in that game. But, as big time players go, there are not many as big as Pierce, who had 36 points and 14 rebounds in a Game 2 win for the Celtics.

Paul Pierce would then score 21 as Boston won their first game at home before defending both home games with a Game 4 win. Pierce had 24 in that win. The Hawks, not to be outdone, would push the series to at least one more game by winning Game 5. However, that was all they wrote as the Celtics took Game 6 to proceed to the second round. Pierce had 18 points, five rebounds, and seven assists in that closeout win. It seemed like he suddenly found the fountain of youth as he averaged more than 21 points in that series.

In the second round, the Celtics were tasked to square off against the young Philadelphia 76ers. Pierce would only have 14 points in Game 1, but his team took that win. Philly would then limit Paul Pierce to merely 7 points in Game 2 as they won the game by one point. Pierce would bounce back big time by leading the Celtics to a 16-point win in Game 3. He had 24 points and 12 rebounds in that outing. It was a series of back-and-forth as the Sixers would win Game 4 on their home floor. In that game, Pierce had a solid outing with 24 points.

Because it seemed like the series' theme was "what you can do, I can do better," the Celtics would win Game 5 by 16 points as they were merely a game away from getting back to the Eastern Conference Finals. Pierce would finish with 16 points in that game as his team needed every point of his production to win.

Not surprisingly, the 76ers would take Game 6 to force a do-or-die situation in Game 7. Pierce would finish with 24 points and ten rebounds in that night. Despite fouling out in Game 7, Pierce contributed solidly with 15 points and nine rebounds as they defeated the younger counterparts to proceed to the Conference Finals.

When they met the Miami Heat back in the second round of the 2011 playoffs, it seemed like the Boston Celtics were too old and too slow to run with three superstars in the prime of their playing years. In the Eastern Conference Finals of 2012, it momentarily seemed like the Celtics could not beat the Heat as Miami took Games 1 and 2. In Game 2, Pierce had 21 points as he tried to battle and defend LeBron James.

When the Boston Celtics got home for Games 3 and 4, they got their championship form and stifling defense back as they suffocated the Heat's trio. In Game 3, the Celtics held a big fourth quarter lead that was trimmed down a bit by the Heat in the fourth quarter. Fortunately, the lead was big enough that they defeated Miami with the strength of Pierce, Rondo, and Garnett's solid games. Game 4 went into overtime as Miami trimmed down another second half lead. But defense was the name of the game in the extra five-minute period as the Celtics held the Heat to merely two points two win the game. Paul Pierce led Boston with 23 points in that game.

Boston would take the series lead by winning Game 5 in Miami. In that match, they stifled the offense of the Miami Heat as the Celtics banked on Pierce and KG for scoring. It was in that game when Paul Pierce hit a dagger three-pointer over the outstretched arms of LeBron James. For that night, LeBron could not handle the truth. Not to be outdone by older veterans, the Miami Heat ran roughshod over the Celtics in Game 6 on the strength of James' 45-point game. Pierce was limited to 9 points in that awful blowout loss. Despite that loss, the Celtics had one last chance to get back to the NBA Finals, but they were one again stopped by the Miami Heat, who began clicking on all cylinders to beat Boston by 13 points. After that loss, it seemed like the Boston Celtics have all but exhausted their fuel reserves for another run at a title. It also seemed like they the days of the Big Three were already numbered.

End of the Big Three, Final Season in Boston

The Boston Celtics would immediately get sour news as Ray Allen, who was a free agent in the offseason, would not sign with the Celtics and decided to join the Miami Heat instead. That officially ended the Big Three era of that generation's

Boston Celtics. Pierce would later comment that Ray Allen was never truly a part of the Big Three. He never bonded with Pierce and Garnett so much as he would often prefer to spend time alone doing other activities. Allen also distanced himself from other Celtics because of his bad relationship with Rajon Rondo.[xv] Nevertheless, Allen was still instrumental in the 2008 title run and the 2010 Finals appearance.

Without Ray Allen in the 2012-13 season, Paul Pierce had to carry the offensive load more than he ever did because of the lack of offensive weapons for the Boston Celtics. He would score 23 points in the first game of the season in a loss to the Heat. On November 3, 2012, he would then have 27 points in a win over the Wizards. Against the same team in their next game, Pierce had 15 points and ten rebounds in another win.

On December 12, Paul Pierce scored a then-season high of 34 points on 11 out of 25 shooting from the field against the Dallas Mavericks in a win. He would then re-establish a new season high when he put up 40 points on the board versus the Cavaliers on December 19. Pierce was already 35, but he was still able to put up 13 of his 16 shots from the field, 6 of 7 three-point shots, and 8 of his 8 free throw attempts.

Later in the season, Paul Pierce had a triple-double game on January 27, 2013. He had 17 points, 13 rebounds, and ten assists in that win over the Miami Heat. He would then have two consecutive double-doubles in the next two games, which were both wins. On February 10, he would then have another triple-double when he put up 27 points, 14 rebounds, and 14 assists. For a moment, Paul Pierce was back to playing his old all-around game when he was still a one-man team in Boston. However, he would not be selected as an All-Star that season particularly because of the mediocre record that the Celtics had.

Despite the setbacks of not making the All-Star team and of struggling to carry the Celtics to the playoffs, Pierce would still try his best to shoulder the burdens. From March 27 to 31, he had three consecutive double-double games. In the middle game of that run, he had another triple-double as he had 20 points, ten boards, and ten dimes in a win versus the Atlanta Hawks. Pierce would then have 24 points and 15 boards in a loss to the Knicks.

In that season, Pierce averaged 18.6 points, 6.3 rebounds, and 4.8 assists while shooting 43.6% from the floor and 38% from beyond the arc. As good as he was on the individual level despite playing at the age of 35, Paul Pierce's Boston Celtics would only get to the playoffs with the seventh seed as they finished the regular season with a record of 41-40. In the first round of the postseason, they were defeated by the New York Knicks in six games as it seemed like that era of the Celtics was coming to a close. Pierce would only average a shooting clip of about 37% in that series.

Short Stop in Brooklyn

Because of the Boston Celtics had a terrible season in 2012-13, the front office decided to pull off a major deal that would jumpstart a rebuilding process for the Green Team while giving Paul Pierce and Kevin Garnett both fresh starts elsewhere. The first move was the trade of Doc Rivers to the LA Clippers in place of cash considerations and a first round pick. On the day of the 2013 NBA Draft, the Celtics swapped Pierce and KG over to the Brooklyn Nets for a package that included Gerald Wallace and Jason Terry among others. The moved allowed Boston to start anew with head coach Brad Stevens and rising star point guard Rajon Rondo.

Paul Pierce and KG were joining a very optimistic Brooklyn Nets team that did not bother with how much cash they were spending to jumpstart a rising fan-base ever since the franchise relocated from New Jersey to Brooklyn. They were paying significant salaries to veteran former All-Star players Paul Pierce, Kevin Garnett, Deron Williams, and Joe Johnson alongside rising young center Brook Lopez. On paper, the team looked convincing. However, three of their starting five were aging while Deron Williams looked like a shell of his former self. To top all of that, the Nets hired freshly-retired Jason Kidd as the head coach of the team despite his inexperience in any coaching position. Nevertheless, the Nets were still poised to contend in the East.

For Paul Pierce, it was not a bitter parting with the team he had spent 15 seasons playing for. He made all 10 of his All-Star appearances as a member of the Celtics. He won a championship in 2008 when he played for Boston. While he may have wanted to retire with the team that drafted him back in 1998, both he and the Celtics knew that parting would be better. The Celtics wanted to rebuild, but Pierce's salary was hampering them from doing so. The Truth wanted to play for championship contenders, but the Celtics were not in the best position to get them to that point. With that, the Boston Celtics expressed their heartfelt gratitude to both Pierce and Garnett as they thanked them and hoped the best for two of the stars that ended the franchise's 22-year title drought.

In his first game as a Net, Paul Pierce scored 17 points in a loss to the Cleveland Cavaliers. He bounced back with a win versus the Miami Heat as he poured in 19 points, five rebounds, and six assists. However, despite all the money the Nets poured in, the team was struggling to win games. Pierce did not seem like his Boston self as he struggled to put up points on the board. He would even miss a few games as age and injuries got to him in the middle of the season.

Things seemed terrible at first as the Brooklyn Nets appeared to be a sinking ship. That was compounded when Brook Lopez went down with a season-ending injury after only 17 games. Though it may sound odd, that was when the Nets' season turned around. All out of options, Kidd moved Kevin Garnett over to the center position as his size and length helped on the defensive end. The odd move was that Paul Pierce was put on the power forward position despite his apparent size disadvantage. But that proved to be the key to Brooklyn's turnaround. Pierce, though undersized, had a lot of strength and experience to bang with opposing power forwards. On the offensive end, he was a mismatch because his quickness and his perimeter game stretched the floor and made opposing big men work harder to cover the perimeter. The small ball worked for the Nets.

On January 1, 2014, Paul had 23 points as he led the Nets to a second win over the Miami Heat. He would then score a season high of 33 points on the in a narrow loss to the Toronto Raptors on January 27. Pierce and the Nets would continue their regular-season mastery over the Miami Heat by winning the third game against them on March 12. Pierce scored 29 in that match. On April 8, he and his squad completed a sweep against the defending champions when he scored 14 in a win. Three days later, Paul Pierce would become one of less than 20 players in NBA history to break the 25,000 point mark. At the end of the regular season, the 36-year-old Paul Pierce averaged 13.5 points, 4.6 rebounds, and 2.4 assists as he helped the Nets secure the sixth seed in the Eastern Conference with a record of 44-38.

Paul Pierce and his group of veterans went on to face the Toronto Raptors in the first round of the postseason. In Game 1, Pierce scored 15 points that included a dagger three-pointer at the end of the match. After hitting that shot, he exclaimed, "That's why they got me here," referencing why the Nets were keen on acquiring the big shot maker. He was instrumental in a Game 3 win as he scored 18 points for the Nets. Despite having 22 points in Game 4, Pierce could not help his team win Game 4. Things did not change much as the Nets lost Game 5. Brooklyn managed to force Game 7 by winning Game 6 by 14 big points. Both Toronto and Brooklyn fought each other almost to a stalemate in Game 7. With merely seconds left, the Nets were leading by one point as Toronto had possession of the ball. Kyle

Lowry attempted a shot that had a chance of winning the game for the Raptors, but Pierce, who was limited to merely 10 points that game, showed why he was clutch on all facets of the game as he blocked the attempt to win the series.

The Nets, who swept the Heat in all four regular season meetings, would face Miami in the second round. However, the playoffs are always an entirely different animal. The Miami Heat were not in the mood to play games with anyone in their quest for three straight titles. The result of their resolve were easy wins over the Nets in Games 1 and 2. Pierce combined for merely 21 points in those losses.

The Brooklyn Nets managed to fight back when they took Game 3 by 14 points. Pierce had 14 points in that game in an efficient 5 out of 10 shooting. However, all the fight left in them was quickly sapped away by the superior Miami Heat team that defeated them in the next two games to proceed to the Eastern Conference Finals. It was a disappointing end for the Brooklyn Nets, who shelled out millions of dollars for a chance to bring a group of veteran All-Stars together for a championship shot.

One Year in Washington

Paul Pierce, a free agent after his short stint in Brooklyn, would look for greener pastures elsewhere as he signed with the

Washington Wizards for a two-year, $11 million contract that had an opt-out clause in the second year. Though he was still an accomplished player at the small forward position, Paul Pierce was at the twilight of his storied career. He could no longer shoulder a whole team like he did in his early years in Boston. However, he was a veteran presence with a lot of experience and leadership qualities. Pierce would be a good fit for a young and talented Washington Wizards squad that was leaning on the likes of John Wall and Bradley Beal for a shot at a playoff team.

With the Wizards, Pierce immediately took the starting small forward position for his ability to lead younger players and for his penchant for hitting big shots when they mattered most. He was an invaluable piece for a rising Wizards team that had a lot of young pieces. The one thing they lacked most was leadership as their best players were too young to provide that. Aside from all the big shots and the timely scoring that Paul Pierce provided, he fast-tracked the maturity of the Wizards.

Paul Pierce began his season by putting up 17 points in a losing effort to a new-look Miami Heat team. He notched his first win as a Wizard in their second game of the season. Pierce had 16 points in that win. He was also instrumental in helping the Washington Wizards to a good 4-1 start through their first five games in the 2014-15 season. Through their first 10 outings, they were 7-3 as Pierce helped in giving a winning culture to Washington.

On November 22, 2014, Paul Pierce had one of his better performances as a Wizard when he put up 25 points and 10 rebounds in a win over the Milwaukee Bucks. On December 8, he would score 28 points in a win over his old team the Boston Celtics. It was in that moment when he moved up to 16th in all-time points scored as he overtook Reggie Miller in that regard. That was merely one game after he went back to Boston to score 16 in a losing effort in front of the crowd that had cheered for him for 15 years.

Paul Pierce was not done in moving up the annals of NBA history. He would pass Jason Kidd for fourth place in most career three-pointers made when he made two three-pointers in a win over the Bulls on January 14, 2015. He finished with 22 points on that memorable night. Pierce would also move to 15th place in all-time career points when he scored 11 points in a losing effort to Charlotte early in February.

Other than moving up in his career totals, Paul Pierce was more or less a role player that could score in double digits for the Washington Wizards that season. The Wizards were contenders for a playoff spot, but they were severely inconsistent and would trade winning streaks with losing stretches. Nevertheless, they finished the season with a record of 46-36, which qualified them as the fifth seed in the Eastern Conference. Paul Pierce averaged 11.9 points and four rebounds while shooting 44.7% from the field.

Paul Pierce and the Washington Wizards were surprisingly good in their first round matchup versus the Toronto Raptors. The Truth showed why he was one of the most clutch players in the NBA as the 37-year old poured in 20 points in 36 minutes of action to draw first blood against the Raptors. Pierce was playing a different role in that game. Toronto fans were heavily booing him after he said in an interview that the Raptors did not have what it took to win a title that year. However, the negativity only fueled him for an explosive game. You never want to get on the bad side of one of the best big-time players in the NBA.[xvi]

Though he would only score 10 points in Game 2, his team won by 13 points. Paul was instrumental in helping the Wizards get an insurmountable 3-0 lead in that series as he went for 18 points on 5 out of 9 shooting from the floor and 4-7 from the three-point line. It was in that game when Paul Pierce once again showed his penchant for making big plays and hitting big shots. He scored 8 points in the final two minutes of the game.

No shot he made was greater than the three-pointer he hit with under 17 seconds left. After hitting that shot, The Truth would shout the phrase, "That's why I'm here." It was only about a year before that when he uttered similar words after hitting a big shot versus the same Toronto Raptors as a member of the Brooklyn Nets. The Wizards chased the fight away from the Raptors as they blew them out of Washington with a 31-point win in Game 4. Paul Pierce had 14 markers in that game as his team swept the Raptors away.

In the second round, Paul Pierce scored 19 points as he helped his team win Game 1 versus the top-seeded Atlanta Hawks. The Wizards would drop Game 2. In Game 3, Pierce was back to hitting clutch shots again. The game was tied at 101 as the Wizards had possession of the ball with only seconds remaining. Pierce received the ball as he was defended by the smaller Dennis Schroder. Using his size and heft, Pierce created space as he rose up and drained a banking buzzer-beating perimeter shot despite having multiple defenders all over him. That shot sealed the win for the Wizards. In a storied career filled with clutch moments, that was the third time Paul Pierce drained a game-winner in the playoffs. They were up 2-1 after that win.

Paul Pierce would score a personal playoff high of 22 points in Game 4, which was a loss for his Wizards. Games 5 and 6 were played tightly. Neither team wanted to give an edge either both game. However, Atlanta proved to be the superior team as they took those two games to win the series. Paul Pierce suddenly disappeared in those games as he was limited to a combined output of only 15 points on 4 out of 16 shooting from the floor. With those losses, the Washington Wizards would bow out of the playoffs in the second round.

Reunion with Doc Rivers, Running with Lob City

Paul Pierce would opt out of the second year with the Washington Wizards to become a free agent in the 2015 offseason. In need of a capable player at the small forward spot, the Los Angeles Clippers took the old veteran for a price of $10 million stretched over three seasons. As Paul Pierce was set to suit up for the LA Clippers, he was reunited with Doc Rivers, the coach that helped him win a title in 2008. Pierce was also reunited with his old stomping grounds. A few minutes from Los Angeles is Inglewood, where he grew up and developed his basketball skills while watching the Los Angeles Lakers in awe.

The Clippers were a good fit for Paul Pierce. That team had the likes of Chris Paul, Blake Griffin, Jamal Crawford, and JJ Redick to carry the offensive load. Athletic center DeAndre

Jordan was handling the rebounding and the defensive duties inside the paint. The only thing that Paul Pierce had to focus on was hitting big shots and perimeter jumpers because he was too old at 38 years old to carry a lot of offensive duties for his team.

In an attempt to preserve his clutch player, Rivers had Pierce playing off the bench at the start of the regular season. In his first game as a Clipper, Paul Pierce scored 12 points to help his team win over the Sacramento Kings. He was relegated to role player duties as the LA Clippers opened the season 4-0. Pierce would hit double digits again in a loss to the Dallas Mavericks on November 11, 2015. He had 10 points in that game. On November 29, he hit 10 points in a win over the Minnesota Timberwolves. On December 12, he had 10 points again in a win over the Brooklyn Nets, one of his old teams. Four days after that, Pierce had 6 points in a win versus the Milwaukee Bucks to surpass the 26,000-point mark. He would become only the 16th player in NBA history to reach that milestone.

In the late parts of December, the LA Clippers would lose Blake Griffin to a hand injury. Without their leading scorer, other Clipper players would have to step up. One of those players were Paul Pierce. The former All-Star forward had a season high of 20 points off the bench in a win over the Utah Jazz on December 26. After that, Pierce reprised his role as a starter when Doc Rivers inserted him at the starting power forward spot. On December 30, Pierce would score 13 points in a win over the Charlotte Hornets. On January 6, 2016, he would deliver 17 points on 5 out of 6 shooting from beyond the arc for another win. A week later, he helped the LA Clippers win their 10th straight game when he had 15 points and nine rebounds against the Miami Heat. On January 16, Paul Pierce became only the 17th NBA player to log in over 45,000 minutes in a loss to the Kings.

Paul Pierce would continue to play the starting power forward position as Blake Griffin was recovering from surgery. Doc Rivers would also rest him a few games as he opted to preserve the 38-year old player's bones and legs in case they would have a chance to play deep into the postseason. Paul Pierce averaged career lows of 6.1 points and 2.7 rebounds while shooting 36% from the floor in his 18th year in the NBA. The Los Angeles Clippers were a playoff team as they were the fourth seed in the Western Conference. As the Clippers marched into the postseason, Paul Pierce was vocal in saying that he would retire immediately if his team wins the NBA title.

Chapter 5: Paul Pierce's Personal Life

Paul Pierce lived and grew up in Inglewood, California. He was but a few miles away from Los Angeles, and his house was a stone's throw away from The Forum, the old arena where the Lakers used to play. As such, Pierce grew up as a fan of the LA Lakers and Magic Johnson. He also idolized Larry Bird and Michael Jordan, though their teams would sometimes give nightmares to his Los Angeles Lakers.

Pierce grew up with a single mom. He never met his father, and still has not. Because of that, his mom Lorraine had to work double jobs as a nurse. Paul Pierce grew up with two older half brothers named Jamal and Stephen. Both of his brothers were also good athletes in their own way. Jamal received a college basketball scholarship, but never got a chance to play in the NBA. Meanwhile, Stephen was an excellent baseball player. He would get an opportunity to play professional baseball with the San Francisco Giants of the MLB. Paul Pierce currently has three children with his wife, Julie. His kids are named Prianna, Adrian, and Prince.

In September of 2000, just when Paul Pierce was about to break out in his third NBA season, he was stabbed multiple times in different parts of his body because of an altercation that happened in a night club. Pierce recounted that he was merely talking to a few ladies before he suddenly realized he was the victim of a stabbing incident. He had to be rushed to a nearby hospital to have his punctured lungs repaired. No other vital organs were damaged thanks to the thick leather jacket he was wearing that night.

Even after the incident, Paul Pierce would suit up for his team just about a month later. He had the best season of his young three-year NBA career at that time. He was also fully healthy as he played all 82 games for the Boston Celtics in the 2000-01 season. Ever the thankful person, Paul Pierce would later help the Tufts-New England Medical Center, the same hospital where he was brought in after the incident, by offering $2.5 million for equipment upgrades. Paul Pierce was more than generous to the hospital and the staff that helped him recover from an incident that not only nearly cost him his basketball career, but his whole life as well.[xiii]

Paul Pierce goes by the nickname "The Truth." Many teams and NBA players have had "you can't handle the truth" moments when Paul Pierce would burn them with his high-scoring performances or with his clutch game-winning shots. But not a lot of people know how he coined that nickname. In 2001, Paul Pierce was in the middle of a breakout season. He and his

Celtics met the defending champions Los Angeles Lakers on March 31. Though Boston lost that game by five points, Pierce burned LA for 42 points. Shaquille O'Neal was so impressed by the young Pierce that he would call him "The Truth" along with some expletives.[i]

Chapter 6: Paul Pierce's Legacy and Future

When you look back at Paul Pierce's career, you will come to realize how much of an unsung superstar he was. Pierce could not make his high school varsity team in his freshman year, and he was almost cut in his sophomore year if not for a stroke of luck. And despite a great college career for the Kansas Jayhawks, nine NBA teams decided to pass on him in the 1998 NBA Draft. Only when the Boston Celtics' original plan of taking Dirk Nowitzki failed did they take Pierce with their 10th overall pick. Nobody expected Pierce to immediately make an impact in the NBA as the second best rookie of that season. He would later spend his early years carrying the Celtics on his back as the only capable player on the roster. Only after four years of playing high-quality basketball would he be named to the All-Star team. After that, he was yet again pushed back into mediocrity as the world was relishing on superstar wing players like Kobe Bryant, Vince Carter, Tracy McGrady, and LeBron James. Paul Pierce became the classic case of a great NBA player playing on a bad team.

Paul Pierce would never get to win an NBA MVP award, and he wasn't even named to an All-NBA Team more than four times in his career despite putting up superstar numbers and carrying a falling franchise on his shoulders. He would never get the recognition that so many peers have gotten. Even if you ask the usual NBA fan about his best five players during the early 2000's era, you might not even hear Paul Pierce's name getting mentioned as Kobe, Shaq, KG, Dirk, Timmy, T-Mac, LeBron, and A.I. would overshadow him more often than not.

Despite not getting the recognition he deserved and the attention befitting him, Paul Pierce survived. Despite often getting overlooked throughout his life, Paul Pierce rose up to become an NBA legend. You look at some of Pierce's peers. Allen Iverson was out of the league in 2010. Tracy McGrady stopped playing at a star level in 2008 and had to retire at the age of 34 because of chronic injuries. Vince Carter, though still an active player, had to transition to being a role player earlier than expected because his athleticism declined. But Paul Pierce survived the test of time as he continued to play at an elite level when he was in his mid-30s.

The reason why Pierce was able to defy Father Time for such a long time was because of the way he played. Even at a very young age, Pierce was never a colossal player. He also was not quick, nor could he jump out of the building. Paul Pierce had to rely on developing his fundamentals as he grew up from being an unheralded youngster to a college basketball standout. Pierce relied on his ability to hit the midrange jump shot. Paul Pierce carved a career by hitting jumpers from the perimeter and from beyond the three-point line. The Truth scored 30 or more points by posting up smaller defenders. The Truth led his team to victories by earning free throw attempts. He did not jump high for jaw-dropping dunks. He did not break his defenders' ankles with his speed or dribbling abilities. Paul Pierce was just simply an NBA player that could score points in the most fundamental way.

Alongside all of his core competencies and honed talents were tons of confidence within Paul Pierce. He did not have the athleticism of Kobe Bryant, Vince Carter, Tracy McGrady, and LeBron James. He could not run the floor as quickly as Allen Iverson. And he could not dominate the paint like Shaquille O'Neal. But Paul Pierce had all the confidence in the world to the point that he always believed he was the best player on the planet. He hit big shot after big shot and made big play after big play all in big-time games because of the amount of confidence he had in himself. Paul Pierce was never afraid to attempt big shots because he always believed he would make every shot that left his fingertips. That is why he was not afraid to play LeBron James point-for-point in the 2008 playoffs. That is why he believed he was better than Kobe in the 2008 Finals. That is why he was able to hit that game-winner in 2012 when LeBron was right up in his face. That is why he was able to hit those daggers and those game-winners as a member of the Nets and the Wizards.

Paul Pierce's style of game has proved to the world that fundamental skills will always get you farther than any other skill in the NBA. He joins the likes of Tim Duncan, Dirk Nowitzki, and Kobe Bryant among others in that regard. By honing basic skills such as the midrange jump shot, the inside post game, and the simple pump fakes, an NBA player like Paul Pierce was able to get far into his career despite not having tons of athletic abilities or size. He is a testament to the world and to younger basketball players that mastery of basic skills should always come above the flashy style of basketball. Years from now, guys like Kevin Durant, Stephen Curry, and James Harden among others, who are all fundamentally sound players, will join Pierce in showing to the world that fundamental mastery of basketball will get you playing the game at a high level even as you age.

Because of his fundamental "old man game" and supreme confidence, Paul Pierce was able to carve a great NBA career worthy of the history books. Pierce was named to the All-Star

Team 10 times in his 15 years with the Boston Celtics. He became a member of an All-NBA Team four times in a career that has spanned almost two decades. Pierce at the 16th place on the list of total points scored in an NBA career as he piled up over 26,200 points in 18 seasons. Best of all, Paul Pierce was able to win an NBA championship in 2008 when he was also named the Finals MVP. You may say that he only earned a title because of Garnett and Allen, but the thing that stands out is that plenty of NBA players have played alongside two other superstars but never won a championship. Paul Pierce not only earned a title, but did it in his first season with KG and Ray-Ray when he barely even knew them. He was also the MVP of their Finals victory. That meant that he was the standout performer among the many Celtics that contributed to that success.

As a member of that Boston Big Three that was formed in 2008, Paul Pierce was still undoubtedly the leader of the team even with an emotional former MVP like Kevin Garnett and a perennial All-Star shooter like Ray Allen in the fold. He regularly led his team in scoring up until the Big Three was disbanded in 2013. Whenever the Celtics needed someone to bail them out of tough situations, no other player in the lineup could create his shots like Paul Pierce could. That is why his other All-Star teammates would be okay with the idea of deferring to him. That is why Paul Pierce was always the hero that the Celtics needed in dire situations.

Where does that put Paul Pierce in the long, storied history of the Boston Celtics? The Celtics have had the pleasure of seeing legendary players like Bill Russell, Bob Cousy, Sam Jones, Dave Cowens, Larry Bird, Robert Parish, and Kevin McHale suit up for the Green Team. But the Celtic player often overlooked is Paul Pierce. In 15 seasons in Boston, Pierce piled up a total of 24,021 points together with 10 All-Star appearances and one NBA title. While he is no Bill Russell or Larry Bird in terms of MVP's and championships, you can argue that Pierce is better than most of those guys mentioned above in terms of what he meant for the Celtics.

Pierce is second only to John Havlicek as far as total career points in the franchise while he was seemingly a one-man team for the Celtics early in his career. He was not Bill Russell, who spent most of his years playing with Cousy, Jones, and Havlicek. He was not Hondo, who won titles with Russell and Cowens. He was not Larry Bird, who won numerous MVP's and championships with McHale and Parish. Paul Pierce was simply just Paul Pierce when he was piling up those points and making All-Star appearances while desperately trying to lead his Celtics to the playoffs as a lone star. It was only when he had the pleasure of playing alongside other stars when he saw tons of playoff success. Had he been teamed up with those guys earlier in his career, Paul Pierce could have won MVP's and more championships. He could have had a more legendary career than other Celtic greats. He would have had the chance of being the best the franchise has ever seen. He would not have been this unsung hero the world knows him to be.

Nevertheless, Paul Pierce is still one of the best players to suit up a pair of basketball shoes not just in the Celtics' history, but in NBA lore as well. When his career is all but done, we will get to celebrate an unsung hero that always contributed in big time situations. We will get to celebrate The Truth that made big shots look natural. We will get to celebrate a man who was never afraid to go toe-to-toe with the best as he believed that he was the best. We will get to celebrate Paul Pierce for who he is as a champion, as a big shot maker, and as a rightful NBA legend.

Final Word/About the Author

I was born and raised in Norwalk, Connecticut. Growing up, I could often be found spending many nights watching basketball, soccer, and football matches with my father in the family living room. I love sports and everything that sports can embody. I believe that sports are one of most genuine forms of competition, heart, and determination. I write my works to learn more about influential athletes in the hopes that from my writing, you the reader can walk away inspired to put in an equal if not greater amount of hard work and perseverance to pursue your goals. If you enjoyed *Paul Pierce: The Inspiring Story of One of Basketball's Greatest Small Forwards*, please leave a review! Also, you can read more of my works on *Colin Kaepernick, Aaron Rodgers, Peyton Manning, Tom Brady, Russell Wilson, Michael Jordan, LeBron James, Kyrie Irving, Klay Thompson, Stephen Curry, Kevin Durant, Russell Westbrook, Anthony Davis, Chris Paul, Blake Griffin, Kobe Bryant, Joakim Noah, Scottie Pippen, Carmelo Anthony, Kevin Love, Grant Hill, Tracy McGrady, Vince Carter, Patrick Ewing, Karl Malone, Tony Parker, Allen Iverson, Hakeem Olajuwon, Reggie Miller, Michael Carter-Williams, John Wall, James Harden, Tim Duncan, Steve Nash, Pau Gasol, Marc Gasol, Jimmy Butler, Dirk Nowitzki, Draymond Green, Pete Maravich, Kawhi*

Leonard, Dwyane Wade, Ray Allen and Paul George in the Kindle Store. If you love basketball, check out my website at claytongeoffreys.com to join my exclusive list where I let you know about my latest books and give you lots of goodies.

Like what you read?
Please leave a review!

I write because I love sharing the stories of influential people like Paul Pierce with fantastic readers like you. My readers inspire me to write more so please do not hesitate to let me know what you thought by leaving a review! If you love books on life, basketball, or productivity, check out my website at claytongeoffreys.com to join my exclusive list where I let you know about my latest books. Aside from being the first to hear about my latest releases, you can also download a free copy of *33 Life Lessons: Success Principles, Career Advice & Habits of Successful People*. See you there!

Clayton

References

[i] "How Paul Pierce Became 'The Truth'". *SLAM Online*. 6 October 2010. Web

[ii] Brooke, Tyler. "Wizards' Paul Pierce Banks in Game-Winning Shot in Game 3 vs. Hawks". *Bleacher Report*. 9 May 2015. Web

[iii] "Paul Pierce". *JockBio*. Web

[iv] "Biography". *Paulpierce.net*. Web

[v] "My Amazing Journey – Paul Pierce". *NBA.com*. 2007. Web

[vi] "Know the Truth: Kansas". *Paulpierce.net*. Web

[vii] "Paul Pierce". *DraftExpress*. Web

[viii] Feeley, John. "Paul Pierce Scouting Report". *Ibiblio*. Web

[ix] Reddy, Sush. "Paul Pierce Scouting Report". *Ibiblio*. Web

[x] Camerato, Jessica. "Paul Pierce Reflects on Sixers' Passing on Him in 1998 Draft." *CSN Philadelphia*. 15 February 2016. Web

[xi] Dwyer, Kelly. "Paul Pierce Doubts He'd Be Drafted in Modern NBA". *Yahoo Sports: Ball Don't Lie*. 18 November 2014. Web

[xii] "The 1998 Draft Heist". *Paulpierce.net*. Web

[xiii] Lenny Carlos. "The Night Paul Pierce Was Stabbed 11 Times". *Open Court Basketball*. 9 February 2016. Web

[xiv] Thomsen, Ian. "SI Vault: How the Celtics Landed Kevin Garnett and Became Relevant Again." *Sports Illustrated*. 31 July 2015. Web

[xv] Kaufman, Adam. "Paul Pierce: Ray Allen Never Truly a Part of the Big Three". *Boston*. 15 April 2015. Web

[xvi] Bohn, Mike. "Paul Pierce Embraces Villain Role, Wizards Steal Game 1". *USA Today*. 19 April 2015. Web

Made in the USA
Middletown, DE
12 December 2018